Detroit Tigers 2020

A Baseball Companion

Edited by R.J. Anderson, Craig Goldstein and Bret Sayre

Baseball Prospectus

Craig Brown, Steven Goldman and David Pease, Consultant Editors
Robert Au, Harry Pavlidis and Amy Pircher, Statistics Editors

Copyright © 2020 by DIY Baseball, LLC.
All rights reserved

This book or any part thereof may not be reproduced or transmitted in any form or by any means, electronic or mechanical, including photocopying, recording, or by any information storage and retrieval system, without permission in writing from the publisher.

Limit of Liability/Disclaimer of Warranty: While the publisher and the author have used their best efforts in preparing this book, they make no representations or warranties with respect to the accuracy or completeness of the contents of this book and specifically disclaim any implied warranties of merchantability or fitness for a particular purpose. No warranty may be created or extended by sales representatives or written sales materials. The advice and strategies contained herein may not be suitable for your situation. You should consult with a professional where appropriate. Neither the publisher nor the author shall be liable for any loss of profit or any other commercial damages, including but not limited to special, incidental, consequential, or other damages.

Library of Congress Cataloging-in-Publication Data:
paperback
ISBN-13: 978-1-949332-72-8

Project Credits
Cover Design: Michael Byzewski at Aesthetic Apparatus
Interior Design and Production: Jeff Pease, Dave Pease
Layout: Jeff Pease, Dave Pease

Baseball icon courtesy of Uberux, from https://www.shareicon.net/author/uberux

Ballpark diagram courtesy of Lou Spirito/THIRTY81 Project, https://thirty81project.com/

Manufactured in the United States of America
10 9 8 7 6 5 4 3 2 1

Table of Contents

Statistical Introduction v

Part 1: Team Analysis

Detroit Tigers: Where Are You Going, Where Have You Been? 3
   Collin Whitchurch, Spring Marie Cullen and Matthew Trueblood
Performance Graphs 7
2019 Team Performance 8
2020 Team Projections 9
Team Personnel 10
Comerica Park Stats 11
Tigers Team Analysis 13

Part 2: Player Analysis

Tigers Player Analysis 18
Tigers Prospects 103

Part 3: Featured Articles

The Baseball Is Juiced (Again) 119
   Robert Arthur
The Moral Hazard of Playing It Safe 123
   Craig Goldstein

Index of Names 129

Statistical Introduction

Sports are, fundamentally, a blend of athletic endeavor and storytelling. Baseball, like any other sport, tells its stories in so many ways: in the arc of a game from the stands or a season from the box scores, in photos, or even in numbers. At Baseball Prospectus, we understand that statistics don't replace observation or any of baseball's stories, but complement everything else that makes the game so much fun.

What stats help us with is with patterns and precision, variance and value. This book can help you learn things you may not see from watching a game or hundred, whether it's the path of a career over time or the breadth of the entire MLB. We'd also never ask you to choose between our numbers and the experience of viewing a game from the cheap seats or the comfort of your home; our publication combines running the numbers with observations and wisdom from some of the brightest minds we can find. But if you *do* want to learn more about the numbers beyond what's on the backs of player jerseys, let us help explain.

Offense

We've revised our methodology for determining batting value. Long-time readers of the book will notice that we've retired True Average in favor of a new metric: Deserved Runs Created Plus (DRC+). Developed by Jonathan Judge and our stats team, this statistic measures everything a player does at the plate–reaching base, hitting for power, making outs, and moving runners over–and puts it on a scale where 100 equals league-average performance. A DRC+ of 150 is terrific, a DRC+ of 100 is average and a DRC+ of 75 means you better be an excellent defender.

DRC+ also does a better job than any of our previous metrics in taking contextual factors into account. The model adjusts for how the park affects performance, but also for things like the talent of the opposing pitcher, value of different types of batted-ball events, league, temperature and other factors. It's able to describe a player's expected offensive contribution than any other statistic we've found over the years, and also does a better job of predicting future performance as well.

There's a lot more to DRC+'s story, and you can read all about it in greater depth near the end of this book.

Detroit Tigers 2020

The other aspect of run-scoring is baserunning, which we quantify using Baserunning Runs. BRR not only records the value of stolen bases (or getting caught in the act), but also accounts for all the stuff that doesn't show up on the back of a baseball card: a runner's ability to go first to third on a single, or advance on a fly ball.

Defense

Where offensive value is *relatively* easy to identify and understand, defensive value is...not. Over the past dozen years, the sabermetric community has focused mostly on stats based on zone data: a real-live human person records the type of batted ball and estimated landing location, and models are created that give expected outs. From there, you can compare fielders' actual outs to those expected ones. Simple, right?

Unfortunately, zone data has two major issues. First, zone data is recorded by commercial data providers who keep the raw data private unless you pay for it. (All the statistics we build in this book and on our website use public data as inputs.) That hurts our ability to test assumptions or duplicate results. Second, over the years it has become apparent that there's quite a bit of "noise" in zone-based fielding analysis. Sometimes the conclusions drawn from zone data don't hold up to scrutiny, and sometimes the different data provided by different providers don't look anything alike, giving wildly different results. Sometimes the hard-working professional stringers or scorers might unknowingly inflict unconscious bias into the mix: for example good fielders will often be credited with more expected outs despite the data, and ballparks with high press boxes tend to score more line drives than ones with a lower press box.

Enter our Fielding Runs Above Average (FRAA). For most positions, FRAA is built from play-by-play data, which allows us to avoid the subjectivity found in many other fielding metrics. The idea is this: count how many fielding plays are made by a given player and compare that to expected plays for an average fielder at their position (based on pitcher ground ball tendencies and batter handedness). Then we adjust for park and base-out situations.

When it comes to catchers, our methodology is a little different thanks to the laundry list of responsibilities they're tasked with beyond just, well, catching and throwing the ball. By now you've probably heard about "framing" or the art of making umpires more likely to call balls outside the strike zone for strikes. To put this into one tidy number, we incorporate pitch tracking data (for the years it exists) and adjust for important factors like pitcher, umpire, batter and home-field advantage using a mixed-model approach. This grants us a number for how many strikes the catcher is personally adding to (or subtracting from) his pitchers' performance...which we then convert to runs added or lost using linear weights.

Framing is one of the biggest parts of determining catcher value, but we also take into account blocking balls from going past, whether a scorer deems it a passed ball or a wild pitch. We use a similar approach—one that really benefits from the pitch tracking data that tells us what ends up in the dirt and what doesn't. We also include a catcher's ability to prevent stolen bases and how well they field balls in play, and *finally* we come up with our FRAA for catchers.

Pitching

Both pitching and fielding make up the half of baseball that isn't run scoring: run prevention. Separating pitching from fielding is a tough task, and most recent pitching analysis has branched off from Voros McCracken's famous (and controversial) statement, "There is little if any difference among major-league pitchers in their ability to prevent hits on balls hit in the field of play." The research of the analytic community has validated this to some extent, and there are a host of "defense-independent" pitching measures that have been developed to try and extract the effect of the defense behind a hurler from the pitcher's work.

Our solution to this quandary is Deserved Run Average (DRA), our core pitching metric. DRA looks like earned run average (ERA), the tried-and-true pitching stat you've seen on every baseball broadcast or box score from the past century, but it's very different. To start, DRA takes an event-by-event look at what the pitchers does, and adjusts the value of that event based on different environmental factors like park, batter, catcher, umpire, base-out situation, run differential, inning, defense, home field advantage, pitcher role and temperature. That mixed model gives us a pitcher's expected contribution, similar to what we do for our DRC+ model for hitters and FRAA model for catchers. (Oh, and we also consider the pitcher's effect on basestealing and on balls getting past the catcher.)

It's important to note that DRA is set to the scale of runs allowed per nine innings (RA9) instead of ERA, which makes DRA's scale slightly higher than ERA's. The reason for this is because ERA tends to overrate three types of pitchers:

1. Pitchers who play in parks where scorers hand out more errors. Official scorers differ significantly in the frequency at which they assign errors to fielders.
2. Ground-ball pitchers, because a substantial proportion of errors occur on groundballs.
3. Pitchers who aren't very good. Better pitchers often allow fewer unearned runs than bad pitchers, because good pitchers tend to find ways to get out of jams.

Since the last time you picked up an edition of this book, we've also made a few minor changes to DRA to make it better. Recent research into "tunneling"—the act of throwing consecutive pitches that appear similar from a batter's point of view until after the swing decision point–data has given us a new contextual factor to account for in DRA: plate distance. This refers to the distance between successive pitches as they approach the plate, and while it has a smaller effect than factors like velocity or whiff rate, it still can help explain pitcher strikeout rate in our model.

New Pitching Metrics for 2020

We're including a few "new" pitching metrics in the book for the 2020 edition, though unlike last year, these numbers may be a little bit more familiar to those of you who have spent some time investigating baseball statistics.

Fastball Percentage

Our fastball percentage (FB%) statistic measures how frequently a pitcher throws a pitch classified as a "fastball," measured as a percentage of overall pitches thrown. We qualify three types of fastballs:

1. The traditional four-seam fastball;
2. The two-seam fastball or sinker;
3. "Hard cutters," which are pitches that have the movement profile of a cut fastball and are used as the pitcher's primary offering or in place of a more traditional fastball.

For example, a pitcher with a FB% of 67 throws any combination of these three pitches about two-thirds of the time.

Whiff Rate

Everybody loves a swing and a miss, and whiff rate (WHF) measures how frequently pitchers induce a swinging strike. To calculate WHF, we add up all the pitches thrown that ended with a swinging strike, then divide that number by a pitcher's total pitches thrown. Most often, high whiff rates correlate with high strikeout rates (and overall effective pitcher performance).

Called Strike Probability

Called Strike Probability (CSP) is a number that represents the likelihood that all of a pitcher's pitches will be called a strike while controlling for location, pitcher and batter handedness, umpire and count. Here's how it works: on each pitch, our model determines how many times (out of 100) that a similar pitch was called for a strike given those factors mentioned above, and when normalized for each batter's strike zone. Then we average the CSP for all pitches thrown by a pitcher in a season, and that gives us the yearly CSP percentage you see in the stats boxes.

As you might imagine, pitchers with a higher CSP are more likely to work in the zone, where pitchers with a lower CSP are likely locating their pitches outside the normal strike zone, for better or for worse.

Projections

Many of you aren't turning to this book just for a look at what a player has done, but for a look at what a player is going to do: the PECOTA projections. PECOTA, initially developed by Nate Silver (who has moved on to greater fame as a political analyst), consists of three parts:

1. Major-league equivalencies, which use minor-league statistics to project how a player will perform in the major leagues;
2. Baseline forecasts, which use weighted averages and regression to the mean to estimate a player's current true talent level; and
3. Aging curves, which uses the career paths of comparable players to estimate how a player's statistics are likely to change over time.

With all those important things covered, let's take a look at what's in the book this year.

Team Prospectus

Most of this book is composed of team chapters, with one for each of the 30 major-league franchises. On the first page of each chapter, you'll see a box that contains some of the key statistics for each team as well as a very inviting stadium diagram. (You can see an example of this for the Milwaukee Brewers on this very page!)

We start with the team name, their unadjusted 2019 win-loss record, and their divisional ranking. Beneath that are a host of other team statistics. **Pythag** presents an adjusted 2019 winning percentage, calculated by taking runs scored per game (**RS/G**) and runs allowed per game (**RA/G**) for the team, and running them through a version of Bill James' Pythagorean formula that was refined and improved by David Smyth and Brandon Heipp. (The formula is called "Pythagenpat," which is equally fun to type and to say.)

Next up is **DRC+**, described earlier, to indicate the overall hitting ability of the team either above or below league-average. Run prevention on the pitching side is covered by **DRA** (also mentioned earlier) and another metric: Fielding Independent Pitching (**FIP**), which calculates another ERA-like statistic based on strikeouts, walks, and home runs recorded. Defensive Efficiency Rating (**DER**) tells us the percentage of balls in play turned into outs for the team, and is a quick fielding shorthand that rounds out run prevention.

After that, we have several measures related to roster composition, as opposed to on-field performance. **B-Age** and **P-Age** tell us the average age of a team's batters and pitchers, respectively. **Salary** is the combined team payroll for all on-field players, and Doug Pappas' Marginal Dollars per Marginal Win (**M$/MW**) tells us how much money a team spent to earn production above replacement level.

Ending this batch of statistics is the number of disabled list days a team had over the season (**IL Days**) and the amount of salary paid to players on the disabled list (**$ on IL**); this final number is expressed as a percentage of total payroll.

Next to each of these stats, we've listed each team's MLB rank in that category from first to 30th. In this, first always indicates a positive outcome and 30th a negative outcome, except in the case of salary—first is highest.

After the franchise statistics, we share a few items about the team's home ballpark. There's the aforementioned diagram of the park's dimensions (including distances to the outfield wall), a graphic showing the height of the wall from the left-field pole to the right-field pole, and a table showing three-year park factors for the stadium. The park factors are displayed as indexes where 100 is average, 110 means that the park inflates the statistic in question by 10 percent, and 90 means that the park deflates the statistic in question by 10 percent.

On the second page of each team chapter, you'll find three graphs. The first is the **2019 Hit List Ranking**. This shows our Hit List Rank for the team on each day of the 2019 season and is intended to give you a picture of the ups and downs of the team's season. Hit List Rank measures overall team performance and drives the Hit List Power Rankings at the baseballprospectus.com website.

The second graph is **Committed Payroll** and helps you see how the team's payroll has compared to the MLB and divisional average payrolls over time. Payroll figures are current as of January 1, 2020; with so many free agents still unsigned as of this writing, the final 2020 figure will likely be significantly different for many teams. (In the meantime, you can always find the most current data at Baseball Prospectus' Cot's Baseball Contracts page.)

The third graph is **Farm System Ranking** and displays how the Baseball Prospectus prospect team has ranked the organization's farm system since 2007.

After the graphs, we have a **Personnel** section that lists many of the important decision-makers and upper-level field and operations staff members for the franchise, as well as any former Baseball Prospectus staff members who are currently part of the organization. (In very rare circumstances, someone might be on both lists!)

www.baseballprospectus.com

Juan Soto LF
Born: 10/25/98 Age: 21 Bats: L Throws: L
Height: 6'1" Weight: 185 Origin: International Free Agent, 2015

YEAR	TEAM	LVL	AGE	PA	R	2B	3B	HR	RBI	BB	K	SB	CS	AVG/OBP/SLG
2017	NAT	RK	18	27	3	1	1	0	4	2	1	0	0	.320/.370/.440
2017	HAG	A	18	96	15	5	0	3	14	10	8	1	2	.360/.427/.523
2018	HAG	A	19	74	12	5	3	5	24	14	13	2	0	.373/.486/.814
2018	POT	A+	19	73	17	3	1	7	18	11	8	0	1	.371/.466/.790
2018	HAR	AA	19	35	4	2	0	2	10	4	7	1	0	.323/.400/.581
2018	WAS	MLB	19	494	77	25	1	22	70	79	99	5	2	.292/.406/.517
2019	WAS	MLB	20	659	110	32	5	34	110	108	132	12	1	.282/.401/.548
2020	WAS	MLB	21	630	92	30	3	35	102	85	123	5	2	.284/.382/.543

Comparables: Ronald Acuña Jr., Mike Trout, Tony Conigliaro

YEAR	TEAM	LVL	AGE	PA	DRC+	VORP	BABIP	BRR	FRAA	WARP
2017	NAT	RK	18	27	135	1.5	.333	0.0	RF(9): -1.1	0.0
2017	HAG	A	18	96	181	8.0	.373	1.0	RF(19): -1.9, LF(2): -0.3	0.9
2018	HAG	A	19	74	222	14.5	.405	0.3	RF(14): 1.1, CF(2): 0.2	1.2
2018	POT	A+	19	73	260	15.4	.340	1.4	RF(14): 1.0, LF(1): 0.0	1.6
2018	HAR	AA	19	35	113	3.6	.364	0.0	LF(4): 0.6, RF(4): -0.5	0.1
2018	WAS	MLB	19	494	125	40.5	.338	-0.5	LF(114): 2.7	3.0
2019	WAS	MLB	20	659	136	49.0	.312	1.4	LF(150): -0.8	4.9
2020	WAS	MLB	21	630	133	43.6	.310	-0.1	LF 3	4.8

Position Players

After all that information and a thoughtful bylined essay covering each team, we present our player comments. These are also bylined, but due to frequent franchise shifts during the offseason, our bylines are more a rough guide than a perfect accounting of who wrote what.

Each player is listed with the major-league team that employed him as of early January 2020. If a player changed teams after that point via free agency, trade, or any other method, you'll be able to find them in the chapter for their previous squad.

As an example, take a look at the player comment for Nationals outfielder Juan Soto: the stat block that accompanies his written comment is at the top of this page. First we cover biographical information (age is as of June 30, 2020) before moving onto the stats themselves. Our statistic columns include standard identifying information like **YEAR**, **TEAM**, **LVL** (level of affiliated play) and **AGE** before getting into the numbers. Next, we provide raw, untranslated numbers like you might find on the back of your dad's baseball cards: **PA** (plate appearances), **R** (runs), **2B** (doubles), **3B** (triples), **HR** (home runs), **RBI** (runs batted in), **BB** (walks), **K** (strikeouts), **SB** (stolen bases) and **CS** (caught stealing).

Next, we have unadjusted "slash" statistics: **AVG** (batting average), **OBP** (on-base percentage) and **SLG** (slugging percentage). Following the slash line is **DRC+** (Deserved Runs Created Plus), which we described earlier as total offensive expected contribution compared to the league average.

One of our oldest active metrics, **VORP** (Value Over Replacement Player), considers offensive production, position and plate appearances. In essence, it is the number of runs contributed beyond what a replacement-level player at the same position would contribute if given the same percentage of team plate appearances. VORP does not consider the quality of a player's defense.

BABIP (batting average on balls in play) tells us how often a ball in play fell for a hit, and can help us identify whether a batter may have been lucky or not...but note that high BABIPs also tend to follow the great hitters of our time, as well as speedy singles hitters who put the ball on the ground.

The next item is **BRR** (Baserunning Runs), which covers all of a player's baserunning accomplishments including (but not limited to) swiped bags and failed attempts. Next is **FRAA** (Fielding Runs Above Average), which also includes the number of games previously played at each position noted in parentheses. Multi-position players have only their two most frequent positions listed here, but their total FRAA number reflects all positions played.

Our last column here is **WARP** (Wins Above Replacement Player). WARP estimates the total value of a player, which means for hitters it takes into account hitting runs above average (calculated using the DRC+ model), BRR and FRAA. Then, it makes an adjustment for positions played and gives the player a credit for plate appearances based upon the difference between "replacement level"—which is derived from the quality of players added to a team's roster after the start of the season—and the league average.

The final line just below the stats box is **PECOTA** data, which is discussed further in a following section.

Catchers

Catchers are a special breed, and thus they have earned their own separate box which displays some of the defensive metrics that we've built just for them. As an example, let's check out J.T. Realmuto.

The **YEAR** and **TEAM** columns match what you'd find in the other stat box. **P. COUNT** indicates the number of pitches thrown while the catcher was behind the plate, including swinging strikes, fouls and balls in play. **FRM RUNS** is the total run value the catcher provided (or cost) his team by influencing the umpire to call strikes where other catchers did not. **BLK RUNS** expresses the total run value above or below average for the catcher's ability to prevent wild pitches and passed balls. **THRW RUNS** is calculated using a similar model as the previous two statistics, and it measures a catcher's ability to throw out basestealers but also to dissuade them from testing his arm in the first place. It takes into account factors like the pitcher (including his delivery and pickoff move) and baserunner (who could be as fast as Billy Hamilton or as slow as Yonder Alonso). **TOT RUNS** is the sum of all of the previous three statistics.

Justin Verlander RHP
Born: 02/20/83 Age: 37 Bats: R Throws: R
Height: 6'5" Weight: 225 Origin: Round 1, 2004 Draft (#2 overall)

YEAR	TEAM	LVL	AGE	W	L	SV	G	GS	IP	H	HR	BB/9	K/9	K	GB%	BABIP
2017	DET	MLB	34	10	8	0	28	28	172	153	23	3.5	9.2	176	34%	.283
2017	HOU	MLB	34	5	0	0	5	5	34	17	4	1.3	11.4	43	32%	.194
2018	HOU	MLB	35	16	9	0	34	34	214	156	28	1.6	12.2	290	31%	.272
2019	HOU	MLB	36	21	6	0	34	34	223	137	36	1.7	12.1	300	36%	.219
2020	HOU	MLB	37	15	6	0	29	29	184	138	28	2.3	12.1	248	35%	.274

Comparables: Zack Greinke, A.J. Burnett, Aníbal Sánchez

YEAR	TEAM	LVL	AGE	WHIP	ERA	DRA	WARP	MPH	FB%	WHF	CSP
2017	DET	MLB	34	1.28	3.82	4.03	3.0	97.7	58	11	47.8
2017	HOU	MLB	34	0.65	1.06	3.08	0.9	97.5	59.6	15.1	49.9
2018	HOU	MLB	35	0.90	2.52	2.33	7.3	97.5	61.2	16.2	51.6
2019	HOU	MLB	36	0.80	2.58	2.51	7.9	96.8	49.9	17.5	48.3
2020	HOU	MLB	37	1.01	2.75	2.95	5.3	95.8	54.6	15.1	48.2

Pitchers

Let's give our pitchers a turn, using 2019 AL Cy Young winner Justin Verlander as our example. Take a look at his stat block: the first line and the **YEAR**, **TEAM**, **LVL** and **AGE** columns are the same as in the position player example earlier.

Here too, we have a series of columns that display raw, unadjusted statistics compiled by the pitcher over the course of a season: **W** (wins), **L** (losses), **SV** (saves), **G** (games pitched), **GS** (games started), **IP** (innings pitched), **H** (hits allowed) and **HR** (home runs allowed). Next we have two statistics that are rates: **BB/9** (walks per nine innings) and **K/9** (strikeouts per nine innings), before returning to the unadjusted K (strikeouts).

Next up is **GB%** (ground ball percentage), which is the percentage of all batted balls that were hit on the ground, including both outs and hits. Remember, this is based on observational data and subject to human error, so please approach this with a healthy dose of skepticism.

BABIP (batting average on balls in play) is calculated using the same methodology as it is for position players, but it often tells us more about a pitcher than it does a hitter. With pitchers, a high BABIP is often due to poor defense or bad luck, and can often be an indicator of potential rebound, and a low BABIP may be cause to expect performance regression. (A typical league-average BABIP is close to .290-.300.)

Detroit Tigers 2020

The metrics **WHIP** (walks plus hits per inning pitched) and **ERA** (earned run average) are old standbys: WHIP measures walks and hits allowed on a per-inning basis, while ERA measures earned runs on a nine-inning basis. Neither of these stats are translated or adjusted.

DRA (Deserved Run Average) was described at length earlier, and measures how many runs the pitcher "deserved" to allow per nine innings. Please note that since we lack all the data points that would make for a "real" DRA for minor-league events, the DRA displayed for minor league partial-seasons is based off of different data. (That data is a modified version of our cFIP metric, which you can find more information about on our website.)

Just like with hitters, **WARP** (Wins Above Replacement Player) is a total value metric that puts pitchers of all stripes on the same scale as position players. We use DRA as the primary input for our calculation of WARP. You might notice that relief pitchers (due to their limited innings) may have a lower WARP than you were expecting or than you might see in other WARP-like metrics. WARP does not take leverage into account, just the actions a pitcher performs and the expected value of those actions...which ends up judging high-leverage relief pitchers differently than you might imagine given their prestige and market value.

MPH gives you the pitcher's 95th percentile velocity for the noted season, in order to give you an idea of what the *peak* fastball velocity a pitcher possesses. Since this comes from our pitch-tracking data, it is not publicly available for minor-league pitchers.

Finally, we display the three new pitching metrics we described earlier. **FB%** (fastball percentage) gives you the percentage of fastballs thrown out of all pitches. **WHF** (whiff rate) tells you the percentage of swinging strikes induced out of all pitches. **CSP** (called strike probability) expresses the likelihood of all pitches thrown to result in a called strike, after controlling for factors like handedness, umpire, pitch type, count and location.

PECOTA

All players have PECOTA projections for 2020, as well as a set of other numbers that describe the performance of comparable players according to PECOTA. All projections for 2020 are for the player at the date we went to press in early January and are projected into the league and park context as indicated by the team abbreviation. (Note that players at very low levels of the minors are too unpredictable to assess using these numbers.) All PECOTA projected statistics represent a player's projected major-league performance.

Below the projections are the player's three highest-scoring comparable players as determined by PECOTA. All comparables represent a snapshot of how the listed player was performing at the same age as the current player, so if a

23-year-old pitcher is compared to Bartolo Colón, he's actually being compared to a 23-year-old Colón, not the version that pitched for the Rangers in 2018, nor to Colón's career as a whole.

A few points about pitcher projections. First, we aren't yet projecting peak velocity, so that column will be blank in the PECOTA lines. Second, projecting DRA is trickier than evaluating past performance, because it is unclear how deserving each pitcher will be of his anticipated outcomes. However, we know that another DRA-related statistic–contextual FIP or cFIP-estimates future run scoring very well. So for PECOTA, the projected DRA figures you see are based on the past cFIPs generated by the pitcher and comparable players over time, along with the other factors described above.

Lineouts

In each chapter's Lineouts section, you'll find abbreviated text comments, as well as all the same information you'd find in our full player comments. The only difference is that we limit the stats boxes in this section to only including the 2019 information for each player.

Managers

After all those wonderful team chapters, we've got statistics for each big-league manager, all of whom are organized by alphabetical order. Here you'll find a block including an extraordinary amount of information collected from each manager's entire career. For more information on the acronyms and what they mean, please visit the Glossary at www.baseballprospectus.com.

There is one important metric that we'd like to call attention to, and you'll find it next to each manager's name: **wRM+** (weighted reliever management plus). Developed by Rob Arthur and Rian Watt, wRM+ investigates how good a manager is at using their best relievers during the moments of highest leverage, using both our proprietary DRA metric as well as Leverage Index. wRM+ is scaled to a league average of 100, and a wRM+ of 105 indicates that relievers were used approximately five percent "better" than average. On the other hand, a wRM+ of 95 would tell us the team used its relievers five percent "worse" than the average team.

While wRM+ does not have an extremely strong correlation with a manager, it is statistically significant; this means that a manager is not *entirely* responsible for a team's wRM+, but does have some effect on that number.

PECOTA Leaderboards

If you're familiar with PECOTA, then you'll have noticed that the projection system often appears bullish on players coming off a bad year and bearish on players coming off a good year. (This is because the system weights several previous seasons, not just the most recent one.) In addition, we publish the 50th

Detroit Tigers 2020

percentile projections for each player—which is smack in the middle of the range of projected production—which tends to mean PECOTA stat lines don't often have extreme results like 40 home runs or 250 strikeouts in a given season. In essence, PECOTA doesn't project very many extreme seasons.

At the end of the book, we've ranked the top players at each position based on their PECOTA projections. This might help you visualize just how a given player's projection compares to that of their peers, so that even if a dramatic stat line isn't projected, you can still imagine how they stack up against the rest of the league.

Part 1: Team Analysis

Part 1: Team Analysis

Detroit Tigers: Where Are You Going, Where Have You Been?

Collin Whitchurch, Spring Marie Cullen and Matthew Trueblood

2019: What Went Right
The Tigers wound up right where most believed they would be entering the season, but how they got there was less predictable than where they went. The pitching staff was actually kind of good! At least, that is, it was good relative to what one would expect from a staff on a team that lost a historic-ish 114 games. The staff had its origins not in 2019, but on July 30, 2015, when the Tigers sent David Price to the Toronto Blue Jays for three prospects. Two of them were Matthew Boyd and Daniel Norris.

Of the two, Boyd's 2019 breakout was both more unpredictable and more pronounced. The 28-year-old has been in Detroit's rotation since 2017, and while they say development isn't linear, Boyd went from really bad two years ago to merely replacement-level last season to one of the American League's best starting pitchers through the first couple of months. He finished with 3.7 WARP, and it was a little surprising the Tigers didn't deal him at the deadline considering his age and their proximity to contention.

Norris joined the surprising Spencer Turnbull to give the Tigers reliable starting pitching more often than not. Together with Boyd, the troika formed a veritable oasis of tolerable pitching amidst the tire fire that surrounded them. Norris was barely above replacement level but is somehow still just 26 years old and finally overcame what has been the biggest hurdle of his career: health. Injuries had limited the lefty throughout his career, and he had only topped 100 innings once in his career entering the season (and even that was just 101 2/3 in 2017). In 2019 he got all the way to the 144 1/3-inning mark, even as his workload was managed down the stretch. Norris's ceiling and what role he would play for a team that is actually trying to win remains unknown, but it has to be reassuring to the Tigers to know they can still include him in their future plans.

Turnbull somewhat surprisingly won a spot in Detroit's rotation out of spring training and pitched effectively throughout the season even as he again battled myriad minor injuries. He rightly (given his pedigree and the team for which he plays) didn't get a lot of attention but had the type of performance that would lead one to believe he can stick in the back of a rotation going forward. Or, at the very least, the back of whatever it is you call what the Tigers' trot out there in place of a rotation.

There were, believe it or not, a few other positives. There's some sick irony to the fact that the 100-plus loss iteration of this franchise had a shutdown closer when contending Tigers teams had struggled to find someone of that sort. Shane Greene rode a superficially dominant first half to an All-Star appearance that was more than just the token "bad team needs a rep" selection and was rightly dealt at the trade deadline. The return wasn't exactly franchise-altering, but the process was right.

Positionally, the Tigers still lack a lot (understatement) in terms of impact, but Niko Goodrum proved to be a versatile and productive contributor, and the fact that players with an undefined future like Jake Rogers, Willi Castro, Travis Demeritte (part of the return for Greene), Dawel Lugo, Harold Castro, Victor Reyes and others were at least able to reach the majors where the Tigers can start to evaluate what they have is something of a positive. It isn't much, but it's not nothing.

2019: What Went Wrong

Miguel Cabrera made $30 million last year and is signed for another $124 million through 2023. Jordan Zimmermann made $25 million in 2019 and will again in 2020. Together, they were worth -0.9 WARP. The presence of these two veterans for lofty sums and zero production is a significant obstacle to overcome, but those two were not in the main what was wrong with the Tigers, nor were they the sole reasons the Tigers lost their most games since the infamous 2003 team.

To say the Tigers spent liberally during the last few years of owner Mike Ilitch's life would be an understatement. It's actually refreshing, in this day of teams seemingly competing for the $/WAR title instead of the World Series, to look back at a team that pushed their chips into the center of the table every year. The problem for the Tigers wasn't that they handed out extravagant contracts, it's that their player development during that same time period completely tanked.

That brings us to 2019. The Tigers have done a lot of build up on their farm during these early years of the rebuild, but the players they're employing in the meantime are, put bluntly, just not of major-league caliber. After Goodrum, Cabrera, and Nicholas Castellanos (traded for an underwhelming package), the hitters with the next most plate appearances on the team included such names as Brandon Dixon, JaCoby Jones, and John Hicks. Dixon was an offseason waiver claim from the Reds and led the team with 15(!) home runs and has a career .690

OPS. Jones now has more than 900 plate appearances worth of below-average production in his career and his one redeeming quality (defense) cratered this year before injury. Hicks has played parts of five seasons in the majors and never achieved a positive WARP.

It's not just overmatched Quad-A types littering the Tigers' roster. The few semi-heralded prospects they planned on counting on in 2019 cratered to horrifying degrees. Christin Stewart was below replacement level when he wasn't hurt, and Jeimer Candelario was so bad that he was sent to Triple-A in early August after compiling a .198/.289/.326 line in 308 plate appearances. The veterans they brought in to soak up at-bats and eat innings weren't any better. Josh Harrison, Tyson Ross, and Matt Moore all pushed the Tigers backwards. That leaves out Michael Fulmer, who hasn't thrown a pitch in a calendar year and whose status going forward is still completely unknown.

Rebuilds, like prospect development, are not linear. But if there are stages of rebuilds, the Tigers are at the "everything is aflame" stage. Help may be on the way, but it's still far off. —*Collin Whitchurch*

Prospect Outlook

The Tigers have quite a few prospects in the farm expected to debut in 2020. Catcher **Jake Rogers** already made his debut last summer. While he struggled at the plate and may not be thought of as a prospect next year, he's likely to be a huge part of the team. Outfielder **Daz Cameron** is very close to the majors despite hitting .214/.330/.366 at Triple-A Toledo. Both Cameron and Rogers were acquired in the Justin Verlander trade; the Tigers would love to see them thrive at the major-league level. **Isaac Paredes**, who split his time in the minors between third base and shortstop, should make the opening day lineup at third, or at least show up a few weeks later. His heavy frame and above-average power will play well in the majors. He doesn't have the range you want from a shortstop, but flexibility in the infield is never a bad thing. Adding fifth-overall pick **Riley Greene** won't hurt the system's status, either.

The most exciting potential 2020 contributors are on the pitching front. **Matt Manning**, **Casey Mize**, **Alex Faedo**, **Tarik Skubal** and **Beau Burrows** are all likely to appear on the 2020 roster at some point during the season. Mize's stuff is ready; each of his pitches are above average, his sequencing is spot on and he has command of both his pitches and the game like I've never seen. Some injury woes will keep him from making the team right out of the gate, but by mid-season he should get the call. Burrows is in a similar boat, although in his case it's less injury-driven and more due to his shaky performance in Toledo that will keep him in the minors until July. Skubal and Faedo seem most likely to be like late additions down the stretch, with Manning granted spot starts as needed. The Tigers have endured a rough few seasons, but 2020 should be the start of something new. —*Spring Marie Cullen*

2020 Outlook

With that surprisingly passable rotation already in place and an impressive bevy of arms on the way, Al Avila naturally turned his primary winter focus to finding players who could hit. Given the team's overall competitive outlook, recruiting free agents is as hard as convincing ownership to open the checkbook when there's so little to be gained. Avila was able to import the division champion Twins' outgoing right side of the infield, though. Jonathan Schoop and C.J. Cron can't turn a historically awful offense into a good one, but it's a start. Austin Romine was an even less exciting pickup, but the team needed some defensive stability behind the plate, and Romine provides it.

Avila kept the outfield and bullpen open for the many players the team had vying for places within each but did make one addition to the rotation: Iván Nova, whose ERA finally spiked in 2019, but who remains a modestly reliable back-end starter. Detroit will still lose tons of games, but a winter of easy, small, non-risky additions should make them much more respectable and watchable. —*Matthew Trueblood*

Performance Graphs

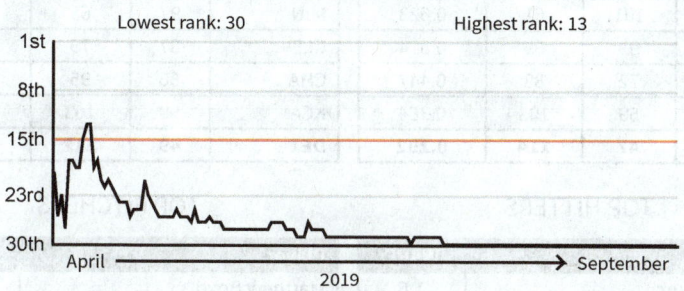

2019 Hit List Ranking

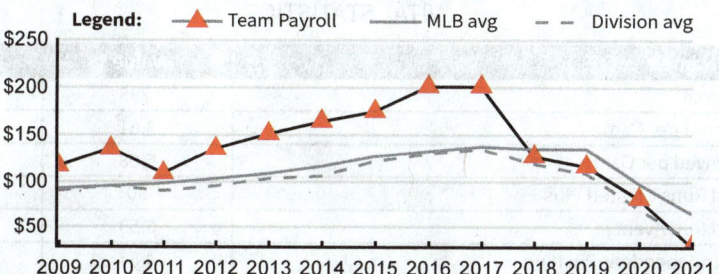

Committed Payroll (in millions)

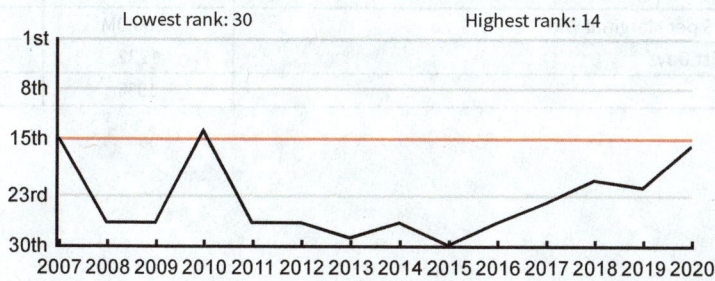

Farm System Ranking

2019 Team Performance

ACTUAL STANDINGS

Team	W	L	Pct
MIN	101	61	0.623
CLE	93	69	0.574
CHA	72	89	0.447
KCA	59	103	0.364
DET	**47**	**114**	**0.292**

THIRD-ORDER STANDINGS

Team	W	L	Pct
MIN	97	65	0.597
CLE	87	75	0.535
CHA	66	95	0.412
KCA	59	103	0.364
DET	**49**	**112**	**0.304**

TOP HITTERS

Player	WARP
Niko Goodrum	1.6
Nicholas Castellanos	1.1
Jordy Mercer	0.9

TOP PITCHERS

Player	WARP
Matthew Boyd	3.7
Buck Farmer	1.1
Spencer Turnbull	0.9

VITAL STATISTICS

Statistic Name	Value	Rank
Pythagenpat	.298	30th
Runs Scored per Game	3.61	30th
Runs Allowed per Game	5.68	28th
Deserved Runs Created Plus	80	29th
Deserved Run Average	5.59	25th
Fielding Independent Pitching	4.87	23rd
Defensive Efficiency Rating	.683	30th
Batter Age	27.5	7th
Pitcher Age	27.9	14th
Salary	$115.7M	22nd
Marginal $ per Marginal Win	$100.0M	1st
Injured List Days	1222	21st
$ on IL	19%	22nd

2020 Team Projections

PROJECTED STANDINGS

Team	W	L	Pct	+/-
MIN	93.4	68.6	0.577	-8
CLE	86.1	75.9	0.531	-7
CHA	82.5	79.5	0.509	10
DET	**69.2**	**92.8**	**0.427**	**22**
KCA	67.8	94.2	0.419	9

TOP PROJECTED HITTERS

Player	WARP
Jonathan Schoop	2.0
Niko Goodrum	1.8
Miguel Cabrera	1.7

TOP PROJECTED PITCHERS

Player	WARP
Matthew Boyd	2.0
Joe Jiménez	1.0
Anthony Castro	0.3

FARM SYSTEM REPORT

Top Prospect	Number of Top 101 Prospects
Casey Mize, #12	4

KEY DEDUCTIONS

Player	WARP
Ronny Rodríguez	0.1
Marcos Diplan	0.0
Matt Hall	-0.1

KEY ADDITIONS

Player	WARP
Jonathan Schoop	2.0
C.J. Cron	1.6
Cameron Maybin	0.9
Austin Romine	0.3
Daz Cameron	0.3
Anthony Castro	0.3
Rony Garcia	0.2
Zac Houston	0.2
Derek Hill	0.1
Isaac Paredes	0.1

Team Personnel

Executive Vice President of Baseball Operations and General Manager
Al Avila

Vice President, Assistant General Manager
David Chadd

Vice President, Player Personnel
Scott Bream

Vice President, Player Development
Dave Littlefield

Manager
Ron Gardenhire

Comerica Park Stats

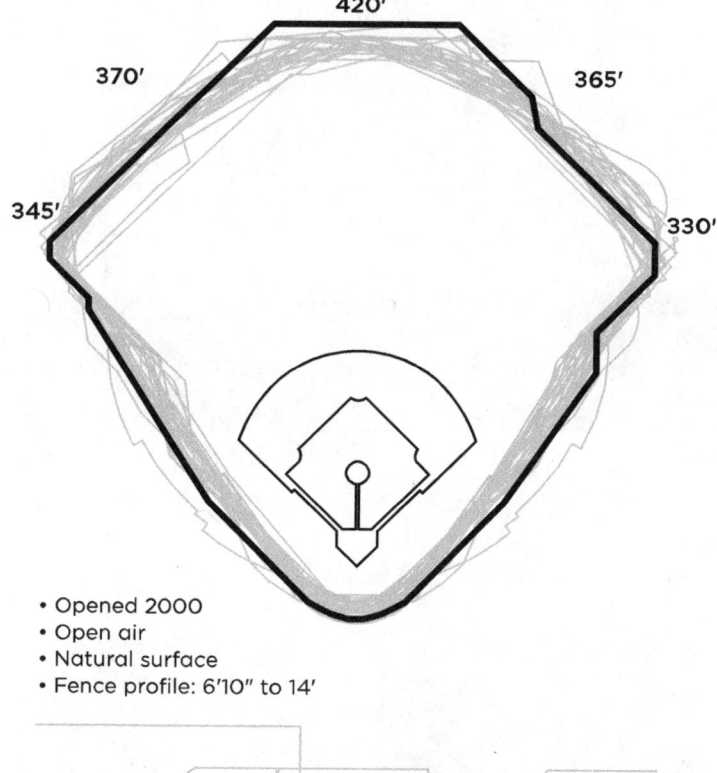

- Opened 2000
- Open air
- Natural surface
- Fence profile: 6'10" to 14'

Three-Year Park Factors

Runs	Runs/RH	Runs/LH	HR/RH	HR/LH
102	104	99	102	97

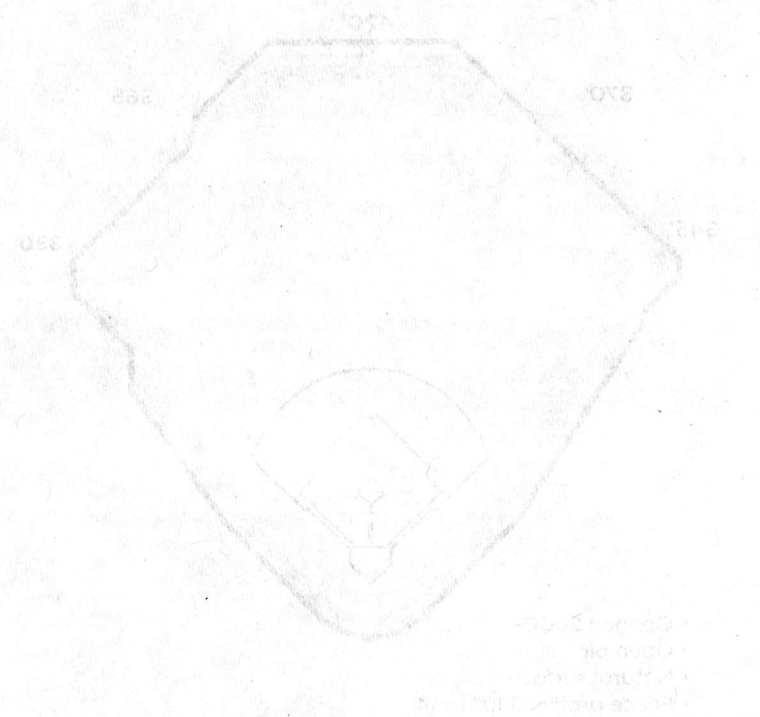

Tigers Team Analysis

The first time Justin Verlander said my name, I took it as a compliment. It was October 2015 and the final day of my rookie year on the Tigers beat for the *Detroit Free Press*, as I stood near the back of the since-renovated visitors' clubhouse at the since-renamed U.S. Cellular Field.

A week earlier, as my long limp to the finish line entered the home stretch, one of my editors levied a challenge: Could I score an interview with the Tigers' resurgent ace and write it up for next Sunday's paper?

The write-up—a story about how Verlander bounced back from core muscle surgery to re-establish himself as one of the better pitchers in baseball—was apparently read by the subject, who pulled up to his locker stall close by.

"About time you wrote a good article, Anthony," he said.

After an eight-month struggle to establish myself in the veteran-laden Tigers clubhouse as a mostly anonymous, sometimes sarcastic, occasionally immature mid-20's beat writer, I had a name.

Following the game, a Tigers loss that cemented the first of three last-place seasons in my five years on the beat, I made my first uncomfortable final-day foray into the clubhouse. The task at hand: Bid adieu to players, coaches and other clubhouse staff with a handshake, and collect as many personal cell phone numbers as possible—"In case I need to get a hold of you in the offseason."

Most players complied. A couple offered their email addresses instead. J.D. Martinez wondered why I decided to ask while he was naked.

But I knew better than to ask Verlander, the celebrity-status face of the Tigers' franchise who had long since directed reporters to get in touch with his agent if they needed anything. I knew better than to overstep my bounds, lest I turn his sweet, sarcastic comment earlier into a sour season-ender for one of my more important relationships.

Relationships. In a word, relationships are what baseball reporting is all about. Relationships are where scoops come from. How the best stories are found. What any reporter worth their salt is judged by, the best of them standing the test of time, much longer than nearly all of us will be writing about baseball.

But as these relationships form, an inherent give-and-take is woven into the fabric between reporters and agents, executives, scouts, media relations officials and yes, players, too. It is not a spoken quid-pro-quo, rather an understanding of everyone's role in baseball's information ecosystem, a respect for what each sector needs and an appreciation when help is afforded.

Verlander willingly handed over his agent's personal cell phone number that day. A year later, after probably a dozen failed attempts, he made contact with me on it.

⚾ ⚾ ⚾

He texted me in early November, well past the due date for submitting ballots. I was a seasoned veteran then—or, so I thought—with two years under my belt and plenty of confidence after breaking big news earlier that offseason about the Tigers picking up the contract option of righty Joakim Soria.

A few of the many, awkward cold calls I placed to agents in laying the groundwork on the beat that first off-season were paying off. But this guy—probably a young, hotshot agent, I imagined—had never returned a call or text. Now, one of Verlander's agents was asking for a favor. In what figured to be a close American League Cy Young Award race, he wanted to get his client some publicity, as if it could change anything—ballots for Baseball Writers' Association of America awards are due before the postseason starts; disclosing them prior to announcement is frowned upon.

To make matters more complicated, I was an AL Cy Young voter. But this opportunity to give—building a relationship with a key person—was too much to pass up.

After hassling him for never answering my correspondence, I wrote up something about the historical perspective of Verlander winning a second Cy Young, which served as a Cooperstown clearinghouse of sorts. With the writing of a future rebuilding process on the wall—one which could send Verlander elsewhere—I was playing the long game, giving to take in the future.

"JV says thanks," he texted.

⚾ ⚾ ⚾

Although you likely can't notice it with the naked eye, the give-and-take in the reporting process is everywhere, showing up on your Twitter feeds constantly.

It's agents leaking information about teams interested in their clients; executives leaking teams' trade interest in their players to influence leverage; smokescreens sent through willing channels—I've certainly been willing before—and narratives pushed by those with agendas.

On a more grassroots level, it's finding out pitching assignments for a traveling scout. Providing them with injury updates and inside opinions on what your team may do. Writing a column when an agent keeps you up all night to convince you that your team should sign their client.

Through these exchanges, trust is built, with the information you give and what you do with the information you take: Nearly two months before the Tigers traded Verlander to the Astros right at the non-waiver trade deadline in 2017, a deal which looks more favorable as the years go on, a top scout from an interested team cornered me with questions about his clubhouse personality.

I didn't do anything with that information, hoping to build trust in the case something did, indeed, go down in the future. Trust waters relationships, helping them grow: Not only do the national reporters work harder than the vast majority of baseball writers, but they've been doing it for quite some time.

And those reporters—unlike the beat writers—have a huge audience, endearing them to agents and executives: "sources" who can communicate their message to the masses with one tweet.

Additionally, some of those national reporters are represented by agents who represent many players. In those cases, it's not hard to trace how certain reporters get scoops.

But for as big as scoops are—and I'd argue they've become less important as the speed of technology has increased—perhaps where beat writers have the biggest influence is locally, with their coverage.

Players read. Executives read. They want good coverage in their own backyard, where they too are trying to build a sense of community with their fans. It's one thing for a national reporter to tweet something out; it's another for a story to be in the newspaper in the clubhouse the next day.

⚾   ⚾   ⚾

The last time Verlander said my name, it was "Fenech," as in, "I told you guys, I'm not talking with Fenech here." I did not take it as a compliment.

This was not unexpected; Verlander was not happy that I wrote a story a season earlier about his claim that the Tigers misdiagnosed his injury years earlier. I was a bad guy. The only one to go ask him about it when he returned to Detroit. Also, a couple solar eclipse tweets years earlier made him feel like a nerd.

I told him that I didn't have much of a choice in the deal—that my editor had told me to come over here and talk to him about it. Plus, there were Tigers folks upset that he had thrown the medical staff under the bus.

But, as a reporter, I did have a choice. Perhaps, I never saw Verlander at his locker. Maybe he blew me off. "I just missed him," I could have told my editors, invoking an executive privilege as part of the give-and-take relationship that is at the core of baseball's information exchange.

Detroit Tigers 2020

There are many players who, in the same boat, had earned that privilege.

But from that Cy Young story—which didn't so much as trigger a response from his agent as the clock ticked down on his time with the Tigers—to the puff pieces and charity stories, the "Justin Verlander is a great guy, just like me and you" narrative I had willfully pedaled in exchange for the smallest kind of take at some point, the imbalanced scales were too much to ignore.

Verlander commented on the injury diagnosis that day. He said a lot more than what I wrote. Then, he deemed the story unnecessary. Then, he said we were off-the-record. Then, in our final comments before that fateful day last season which had me standing outside the clubhouse, I explained to him what was once explained to me, about how you break news in this industry. "I understand you don't want this story written," I told him. "But there's a give-and-take with all of this; you, agents, executives, everybody. And I've been giving for five years now, and, look...."

Verlander took my business card. I told him my deadline. That if he wanted to add anything to the quote, text me. That I'd love to keep in touch, that he's an important guy in Tigers history. He never gave me a text.

—*Anthony Fenech is a Tigers beat reporter for the Detroit Free Press.*

Part 2: Player Analysis

Detroit Tigers 2020

PLAYER COMMENTS WITH GRAPHS

Gordon Beckham INF
Born: 09/16/86 Age: 33 Bats: R Throws: R
Height: 6'0" Weight: 190 Origin: Round 1, 2008 Draft (#8 overall)

YEAR	TEAM	LVL	AGE	PA	R	2B	3B	HR	RBI	BB	K	SB	CS	AVG/OBP/SLG
2017	TAC	AAA	30	355	37	16	0	9	45	20	58	3	2	.262/.313/.393
2017	SEA	MLB	30	18	2	0	0	0	0	1	2	1	0	.176/.222/.176
2018	TAC	AAA	31	425	64	24	1	10	51	57	52	6	2	.302/.400/.458
2018	SEA	MLB	31	50	3	1	0	0	1	4	11	1	0	.182/.250/.205
2019	DET	MLB	32	240	29	13	2	6	15	13	68	3	1	.215/.271/.372
2020	DET	MLB	33	251	22	12	1	6	25	18	64	2	1	.208/.276/.337

Comparables: Cliff Pennington, Vance Law, Terry Shumpert

Beckham is the type of player who looks and feels like he'll be in the league until he's 40, in part because he'll basically accept any pittance of playing time you have for him. (That, and he already plays like that age.) He's the quintessential soft-spoken infielder gallivanting about from team to team, as long as he's somewhere on the diamond. Triple-A is fine, too, because it beats the alternative. He broke camp with the Tigers last year because most of his middle-infield competition was still on the vine, making him an upgrade due to the fact that he's not going to make "rookie mistakes." He just won't hit or make highlight plays. His extant march into Bloomquistian status does not have an ending in sight.

YEAR	TEAM	LVL	AGE	PA	DRC+	VORP	BABIP	BRR	FRAA	WARP
2017	TAC	AAA	30	355	85	8.2	.293	1.4	2B(63): -4.5, 3B(7): -0.8	0.0
2017	SEA	MLB	30	18	87	-1.9	.200	0.2	2B(5): 0.0, SS(4): -0.8	0.0
2018	TAC	AAA	31	425	125	28.9	.326	1.6	2B(32): -0.6, SS(27): -0.5	3.1
2018	SEA	MLB	31	50	82	-1.6	.242	0.3	2B(13): 1.4, 3B(6): 0.2	0.3
2019	DET	MLB	32	240	66	-1.9	.282	0.0	2B(39): 0.3, SS(18): -1.6	-0.3
2020	DET	MLB	33	251	63	-4.0	.263	0.1	2B 0, SS 0	-0.4

Gordon Beckham, continued

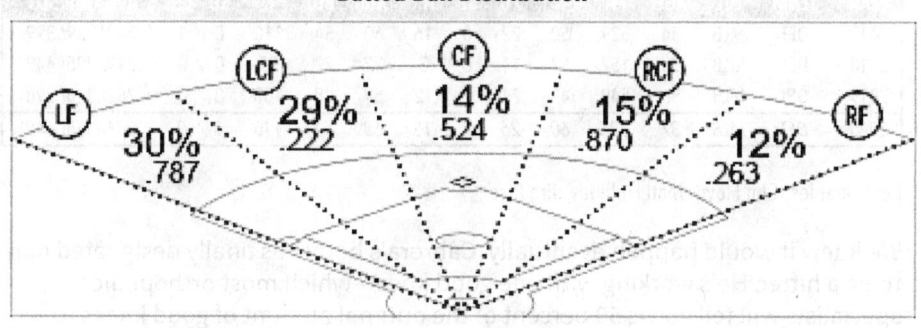

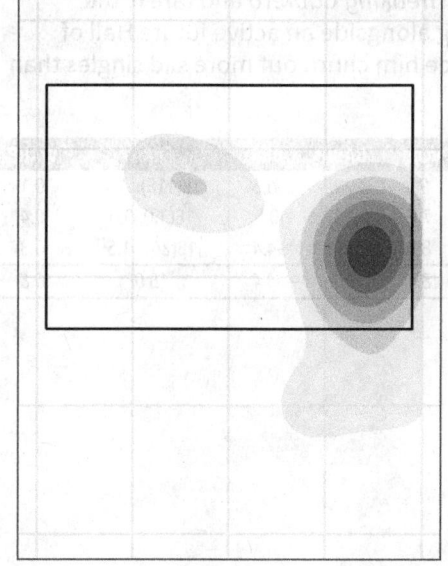
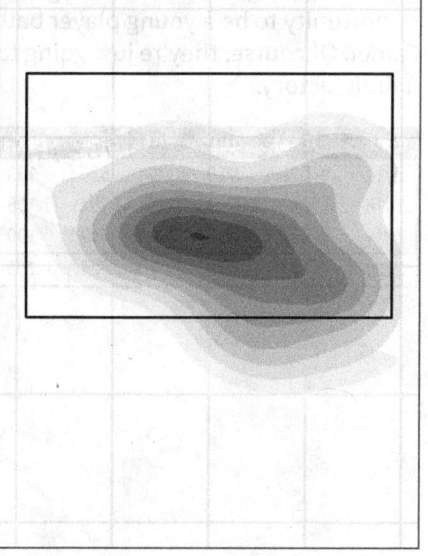

Tigers Player Analysis - 19

Detroit Tigers 2020

Miguel Cabrera   DH
Born: 04/18/83   Age: 37   Bats: R   Throws: R
Height: 6'4"   Weight: 249   Origin: International Free Agent, 1999

YEAR	TEAM	LVL	AGE	PA	R	2B	3B	HR	RBI	BB	K	SB	CS	AVG/OBP/SLG
2017	DET	MLB	34	529	50	22	0	16	60	54	110	0	1	.249/.329/.399
2018	DET	MLB	35	157	17	11	0	3	22	22	27	0	0	.299/.395/.448
2019	DET	MLB	36	549	41	21	0	12	59	48	108	0	0	.282/.346/.398
2020	DET	MLB	37	525	60	26	1	15	63	51	110	1	0	.286/.358/.440

Comparables: Cliff Floyd, Matt Holliday, Jim Rice

We knew it would happen eventually. Cabrera's body has finally designated him to be a hitter. He's working with one good knee—which most orthopedic specialists will tell you is 50 percent of the optimal amount of good knees to play sports—and is learning to slug with just upper body brawn, which you might remember was sapped a bit from his ruptured biceps in 2018. Hitting double-digit dingers might be a chore for him from here on out. His biggest value to the Tigers remains being *Miguel freaking Cabrera* and rare is the opportunity to be a young player batting alongside an active future Hall of Famer. Of course, they're just going to see him churn out more sad singles than a Kraft factory.

YEAR	TEAM	LVL	AGE	PA	DRC+	VORP	BABIP	BRR	FRAA	WARP
2017	DET	MLB	34	529	103	-9.8	.292	-6.6	1B(115): -1.7	0.1
2018	DET	MLB	35	157	108	7.0	.352	0.5	1B(32): 0.0	0.4
2019	DET	MLB	36	549	100	8.6	.336	-4.4	1B(26): -1.5	0.3
2020	DET	MLB	37	525	108	8.1	.346	-3.4	1B 0	0.8

Miguel Cabrera, continued

Batted Ball Distribution

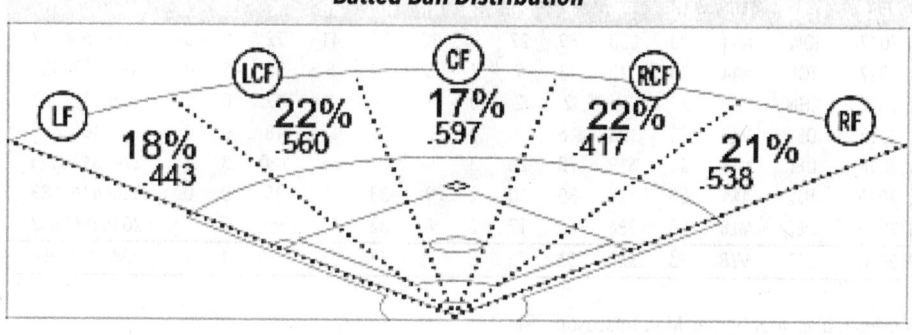

Strike Zone vs LHP   **Strike Zone vs RHP**

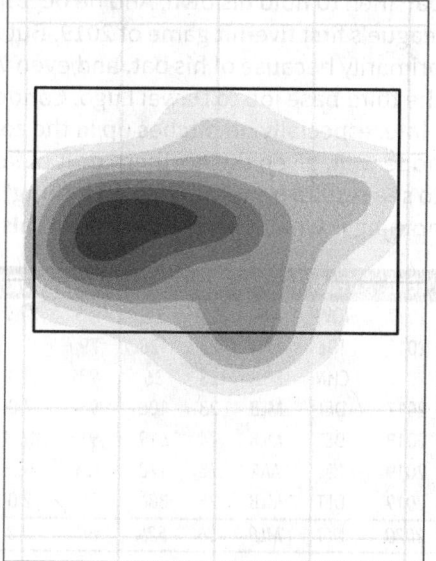

Detroit Tigers 2020

Jeimer Candelario CI
Born: 11/24/93 Age: 26 Bats: B Throws: R
Height: 6'1" Weight: 221 Origin: International Free Agent, 2010

YEAR	TEAM	LVL	AGE	PA	R	2B	3B	HR	RBI	BB	K	SB	CS	AVG/OBP/SLG
2017	IOW	AAA	23	330	39	27	3	12	52	41	72	0	0	.266/.361/.507
2017	TOL	AAA	23	128	13	9	1	3	19	5	32	1	0	.264/.297/.430
2017	CHN	MLB	23	36	2	2	0	1	3	1	12	0	0	.152/.222/.303
2017	DET	MLB	23	106	16	7	0	2	13	12	18	0	0	.330/.406/.468
2018	DET	MLB	24	619	78	28	3	19	54	66	160	3	2	.224/.317/.393
2019	TOL	AAA	25	178	30	10	2	9	33	22	35	0	0	.320/.416/.588
2019	DET	MLB	25	386	33	17	2	8	32	43	99	3	1	.203/.306/.337
2020	DET	MLB	26	525	56	23	3	16	61	55	130	1	1	.224/.314/.394

Comparables: Mat Gamel, Matt Tuiasosopo, Rio Ruiz

In a Tigers lineup filled with more hackers than an audition line for the 1995 box office smash thriller *The Net*, Candelario was expected to be one of the rare batsmen to hold his own. And he began with a bang, recording the entire league's first five-hit game of 2019. But his summer was marred with demotions, primarily because of his bat, and even when he crawled his way back up he lost the third base job to Dawel Lugo. Candelario struggled from both sides of the plate, especially on pitches up in the zone—an aspect of his game that doesn't bode well, given the northern drift of fastballs across the league. At 26, we've yet to see results from the "one sure thing" the Tigers had to offer, further proving nothing is what it seems, which was also the point in *The Net*. (Probably.)

YEAR	TEAM	LVL	AGE	PA	DRC+	VORP	BABIP	BRR	FRAA	WARP
2017	IOW	AAA	23	330	125	22.9	.315	-4.5	3B(70): 5.0, 1B(16): -0.7	2.1
2017	TOL	AAA	23	128	79	1.1	.333	-1.9	3B(28): -1.5	-0.2
2017	CHN	MLB	23	36	98	-1.1	.200	0.2	3B(9): 0.9, 1B(1): 0.0	0.2
2017	DET	MLB	23	106	95	7.0	.392	0.2	3B(27): -2.4	0.1
2018	DET	MLB	24	619	91	16.4	.279	-2.4	3B(140): -4.1	0.9
2019	TOL	AAA	25	178	154	18.5	.367	-1.4	3B(30): 0.1, 1B(7): -0.4	1.5
2019	DET	MLB	25	386	78	2.0	.262	-1.0	3B(69): -1.0, 1B(20): -0.2	0.0
2020	DET	MLB	26	525	88	3.3	.276	-1.0	3B 0, 1B 0	0.3

Jeimer Candelario, continued

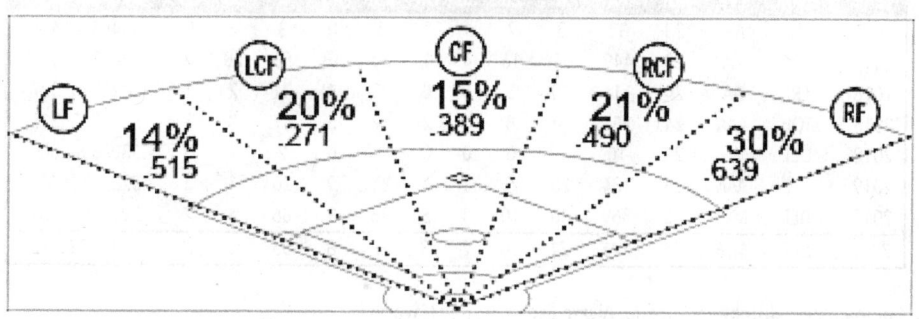

Batted Ball Distribution

Strike Zone vs LHP   **Strike Zone vs RHP**

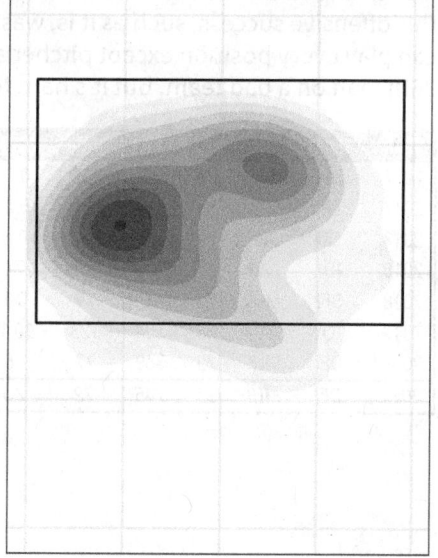

Detroit Tigers 2020

Harold Castro UT

Born: 11/30/93 Age: 26 Bats: L Throws: R
Height: 6'0" Weight: 180 Origin: International Free Agent, 2011

YEAR	TEAM	LVL	AGE	PA	R	2B	3B	HR	RBI	BB	K	SB	CS	AVG/OBP/SLG
2017	LAK	A+	23	33	3	2	1	0	3	0	3	2	0	.364/.364/.485
2017	ERI	AA	23	449	51	16	4	1	30	18	53	20	9	.290/.325/.355
2018	ERI	AA	24	116	10	5	0	0	10	4	21	2	1	.282/.310/.327
2018	TOL	AAA	24	251	24	8	0	2	19	5	47	3	3	.257/.270/.315
2018	DET	MLB	24	10	2	0	0	0	0	0	2	1	0	.300/.300/.300
2019	TOL	AAA	25	134	20	5	1	4	25	9	26	1	3	.328/.371/.484
2019	DET	MLB	25	369	30	10	4	5	38	9	86	4	2	.291/.305/.384
2020	DET	MLB	26	245	21	10	2	3	22	8	55	6	3	.265/.293/.362

Comparables: Humberto Arteaga, Alvaro Espinoza, Rey Navarro

Now there's a batting line out of another era. Castro BABIP'd his way to a perfectly respectable batting average despite taking a walk only about twice a month and rarely hitting the ball hard. Suffice to say, we're extremely skeptical this offensive success, such as it is, was anything other than a random fluke. He can play every position except pitcher and catcher, so you can do worse for a 26th man on a bad team, but it's hard to see much upside here.

YEAR	TEAM	LVL	AGE	PA	DRC+	VORP	BABIP	BRR	FRAA	WARP
2017	LAK	A+	23	33	132	0.0	.400	-0.2	2B(6): 0.6, SS(1): 0.2	0.2
2017	ERI	AA	23	449	84	6.2	.326	1.0	CF(44): -2.9, 2B(42): 0.3	0.4
2018	ERI	AA	24	116	78	-0.6	.344	0.1	2B(14): -1.6, 3B(8): 0.9	0.0
2018	TOL	AAA	24	251	65	-5.4	.309	1.0	3B(30): -0.1, SS(22): -1.7	-0.4
2018	DET	MLB	24	10	79	-0.1	.375	-0.1	SS(4): 0.1, 2B(2): 0.0	0.0
2019	TOL	AAA	25	134	123	10.1	.387	1.6	2B(23): -1.0, 1B(2): 0.1	0.9
2019	DET	MLB	25	369	77	1.6	.367	-2.8	2B(34): -2.1, CF(30): 0.0	-0.4
2020	DET	MLB	26	245	72	-2.5	.335	-1.4	3B 1, CF 0	-0.3

Harold Castro, continued

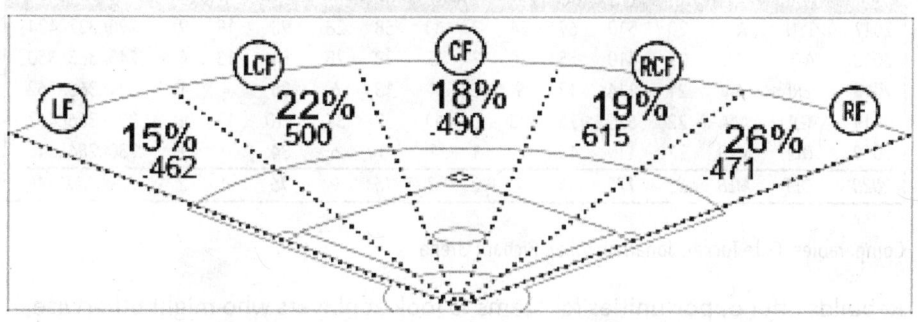

Strike Zone vs LHP

Strike Zone vs RHP

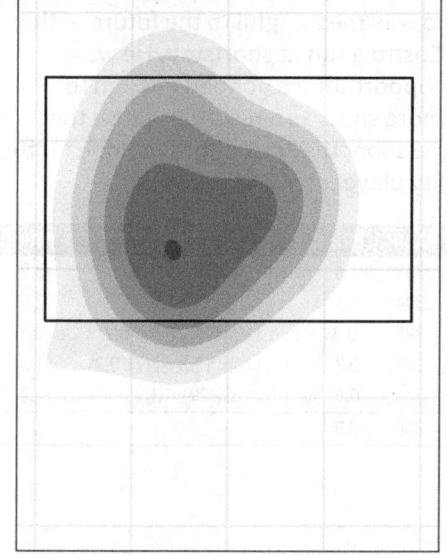
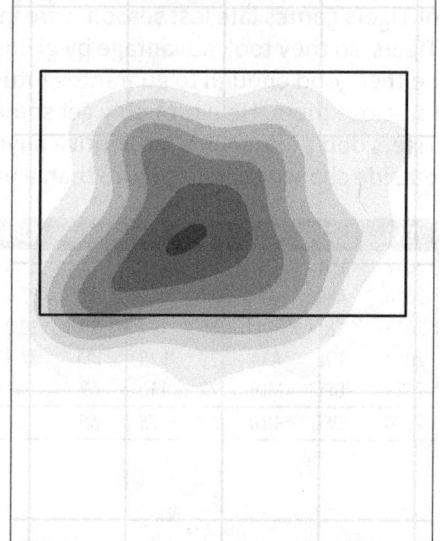

Detroit Tigers 2020

Willi Castro SS
Born: 04/24/97   Age: 23   Bats: B   Throws: R
Height: 6'1"   Weight: 205   Origin: International Free Agent, 2013

YEAR	TEAM	LVL	AGE	PA	R	2B	3B	HR	RBI	BB	K	SB	CS	AVG/OBP/SLG
2017	LYN	A+	20	510	69	24	3	11	58	28	90	19	9	.290/.337/.424
2018	AKR	AA	21	410	55	20	2	5	39	28	84	13	4	.245/.303/.350
2018	ERI	AA	21	114	12	9	2	4	13	6	25	4	1	.324/.366/.562
2019	TOL	AAA	22	525	75	28	8	11	62	37	110	17	4	.301/.366/.467
2019	DET	MLB	22	110	10	6	1	1	8	6	34	0	1	.230/.284/.340
2020	DET	MLB	23	175	15	7	2	3	16	9	46	4	2	.229/.280/.348

Comparables: Cole Tucker, Jonathan Villar, Richard Ureña

Rebuilds offer opportunities for teams to look at players who might otherwise never get a clean shot at starting time. Castro has projected as a utility infielder dating back to his time in the Cleveland system. He's a switch-hitter with a bit of pop who can play shortstop, so he has some things going for him—just not enough that you would usually make room for him in the lineup. The outcome of Tigers games late last season were in no way meaningful to the future of the Tigers, so they took advantage by giving Castro a run at shortstop. He was neither good enough to guarantee future opportunities nor bad enough to foreclose them. He'll probably get some more shots as a result. Because the Tigers don't rate to be competitive anytime soon, they can afford to hope for the outside chance that he's more than a utility player.

YEAR	TEAM	LVL	AGE	PA	DRC+	VORP	BABIP	BRR	FRAA	WARP
2017	LYN	A+	20	510	119	33.6	.336	1.6	SS(122): 5.0	3.9
2018	AKR	AA	21	410	97	17.4	.304	1.3	SS(96): 7.5	2.6
2018	ERI	AA	21	114	99	10.0	.395	-0.8	SS(10): 0.7, 2B(9): -0.2	0.4
2019	TOL	AAA	22	525	111	37.4	.369	0.3	SS(110): -15.3, 2B(7): 0.2	1.6
2019	DET	MLB	22	110	69	0.8	.333	0.9	SS(29): 1.1	0.3
2020	DET	MLB	23	175	65	-1.1	.300	0.3	SS 0	-0.1

Willi Castro, continued

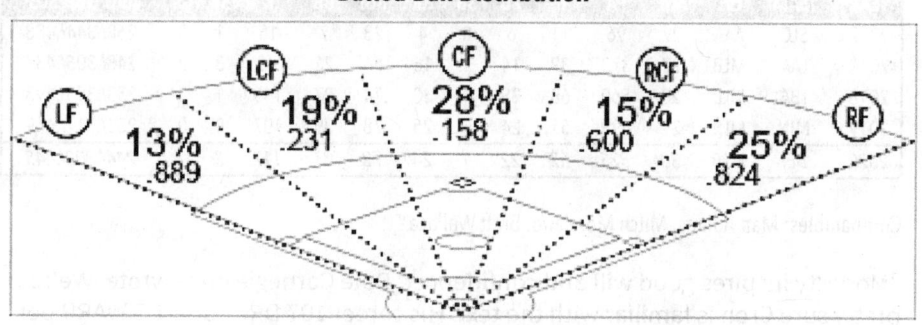

Batted Ball Distribution

Strike Zone vs LHP   **Strike Zone vs RHP**

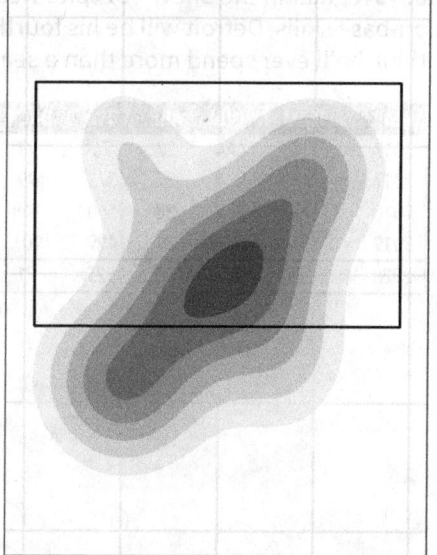

Detroit Tigers 2020

C.J. Cron 1B
Born: 01/05/90   Age: 30   Bats: R   Throws: R
Height: 6'4"   Weight: 235   Origin: Round 1, 2011 Draft (#17 overall)

YEAR	TEAM	LVL	AGE	PA	R	2B	3B	HR	RBI	BB	K	SB	CS	AVG/OBP/SLG
2017	SLC	AAA	27	96	11	6	0	4	23	7	15	1	0	.268/.344/.488
2017	LAA	MLB	27	373	39	14	1	16	56	22	96	3	2	.248/.305/.437
2018	TBA	MLB	28	560	68	28	1	30	74	37	145	1	2	.253/.323/.493
2019	MIN	MLB	29	499	51	24	0	25	78	29	107	0	0	.253/.311/.469
2020	DET	MLB	30	525	62	22	1	24	72	31	117	3	2	.244/.302/.445

Comparables: Matt Adams, Mitch Moreland, Brett Wallace

"Modesty inspires good will and confidence," Dale Carnegie once wrote. We're pretty sure Cron is familiar with the text. His career 107 DRC+ and 1.5 WARP per 162 games are the definition of replaceable-yet-acceptable production for a big-league first baseman. Certainly he's managed to win enough friends and influence enough people to remain employed throughout his 20s as a most-days regular in the Show—despite weak-side platoon traits and below-average on-base skills. Detroit will be his fourth team in four years; there's no reason to think he'll ever spend more than a season with a team again.

YEAR	TEAM	LVL	AGE	PA	DRC+	VORP	BABIP	BRR	FRAA	WARP
2017	SLC	AAA	27	96	99	3.2	.273	0.0	1B(19): 0.9	0.2
2017	LAA	MLB	27	373	99	2.7	.296	-2.1	1B(98): 4.1	0.7
2018	TBA	MLB	28	560	118	17.6	.293	-3.5	1B(61): 2.6	1.9
2019	MIN	MLB	29	499	101	8.3	.277	-2.6	1B(117): 8.0	1.3
2020	DET	MLB	30	525	91	1.0	.275	-2.3	1B 7	0.8

C.J. Cron, continued

Batted Ball Distribution

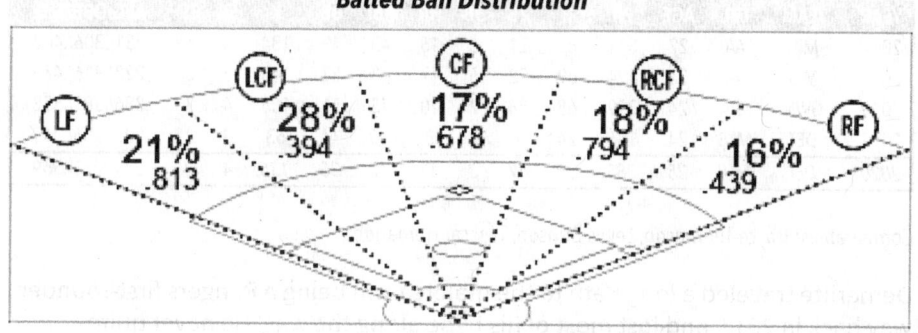

Strike Zone vs LHP

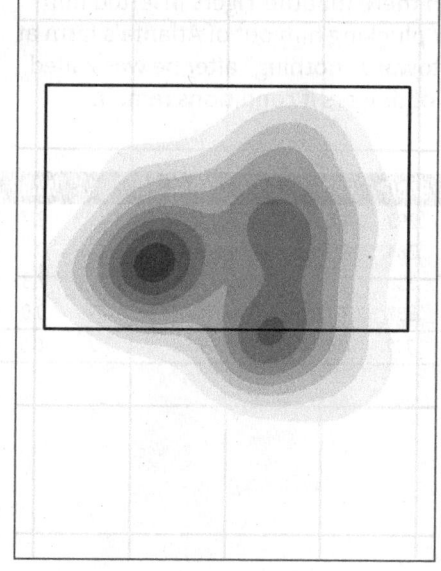

Strike Zone vs RHP

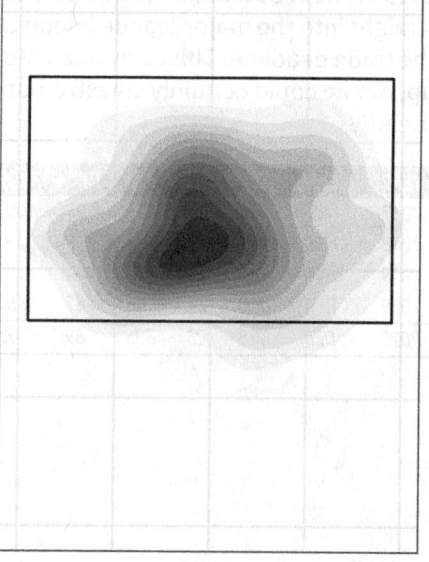

Detroit Tigers 2020

Travis Demeritte   RF
Born: 09/30/94   Age: 25   Bats: R   Throws: R
Height: 6'0"   Weight: 180   Origin: Round 1, 2013 Draft (#30 overall)

YEAR	TEAM	LVL	AGE	PA	R	2B	3B	HR	RBI	BB	K	SB	CS	AVG/OBP/SLG
2017	MIS	AA	22	511	62	21	6	15	45	49	134	5	7	.231/.306/.402
2018	MIS	AA	23	494	69	22	5	17	63	57	140	6	2	.222/.316/.416
2019	GWN	AAA	24	399	68	28	2	20	73	51	106	4	3	.286/.387/.558
2019	DET	MLB	24	186	24	7	2	3	10	14	63	3	0	.225/.286/.343
2020	DET	MLB	25	385	38	17	3	11	42	35	135	4	2	.211/.288/.369

Comparables: Trayce Thompson, Lewis Brinson, Teoscar Hernández

Demeritte traveled a long path to the majors from being a Rangers first-rounder way back in 2013, and lost most of his hype along the way. He never quite developed much of a hit tool, and a year ago looked like he might be stalling out in Double-A. But things turned around when his all-or-nothing power game turned out to be particularly well-suited for the launch-a-ball bonanza known as 2019 Triple-A baseball. He showed enough there that the Tigers inserted him straight into the major-league lineup after plucking him out of Atlanta's farm at the trade deadline. Things trended more toward "nothing" after he was called up, but he could certainly smash a bunch of dingers if conditions remain friendly.

YEAR	TEAM	LVL	AGE	PA	DRC+	VORP	BABIP	BRR	FRAA	WARP
2017	MIS	AA	22	511	97	19.5	.293	1.8	2B(77): 7.8, 3B(43): 1.4	2.7
2018	MIS	AA	23	494	104	19.5	.284	-2.2	LF(119): -5.9, 3B(1): 0.1	0.6
2019	GWN	AAA	24	399	136	29.7	.358	0.0	LF(38): 0.1, RF(36): -2.0	2.3
2019	DET	MLB	24	186	62	-5.0	.337	1.7	RF(47): 3.8	0.0
2020	DET	MLB	25	385	69	-7.3	.309	0.1	RF 2	-0.5

Travis Demeritte, continued

Batted Ball Distribution

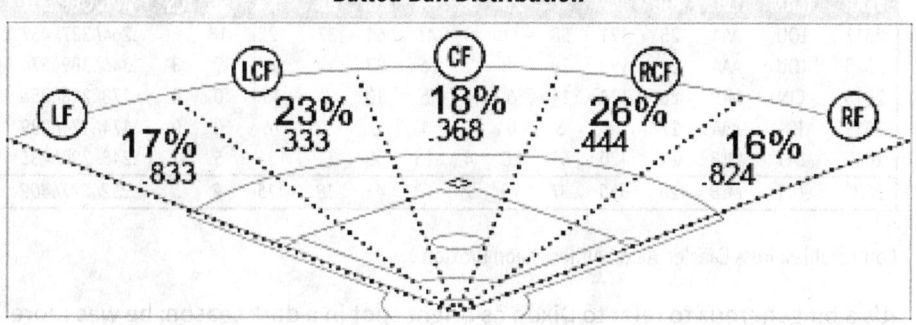

Strike Zone vs LHP **Strike Zone vs RHP**

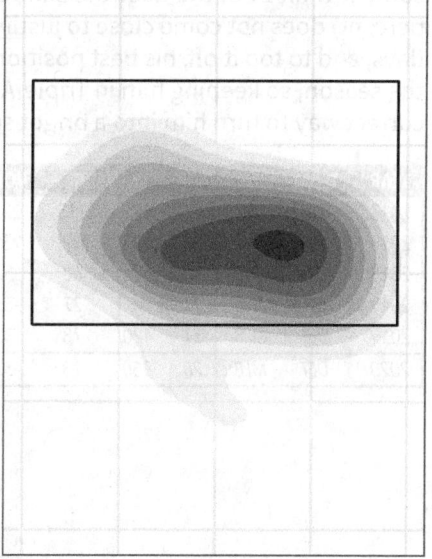

Detroit Tigers 2020

Brandon Dixon   UT

Born: 01/29/92   Age: 28   Bats: R   Throws: R
Height: 6'2"   Weight: 215   Origin: Round 3, 2013 Draft (#92 overall)

YEAR	TEAM	LVL	AGE	PA	R	2B	3B	HR	RBI	BB	K	SB	CS	AVG/OBP/SLG
2017	LOU	AAA	25	491	58	31	3	16	64	37	125	18	8	.264/.327/.457
2018	LOU	AAA	26	193	28	18	2	6	23	12	54	9	3	.346/.389/.570
2018	CIN	MLB	26	124	14	6	0	5	10	6	43	0	0	.178/.218/.356
2019	TOL	AAA	27	46	6	0	0	1	3	0	16	0	0	.174/.174/.239
2019	DET	MLB	27	420	41	20	4	15	52	21	136	5	1	.248/.290/.435
2020	DET	MLB	28	350	37	15	2	13	43	18	115	9	3	.232/.277/.409

Comparables: Russ Canzler, Aaron Altherr, Keon Broxton

It's a bit generous to refer to Dixon as bright spot in a dark season; he was more like a bike reflector in a black hole. Dixon's 15 home runs were the fewest for a team leader since the Padres in 2014, a year in which dingers were way down and definitely not a year where the persons sitting on either side of you somehow hit 27 of them for the Minnesota Twins. His strikeout rate (32.4 percent) does not come close to justifying having him run into one every 10 days, and to top it off, his best position is first base. Dixon had a dismal finish to the season, so keeping him in Triple-A until he hits a hot streak could be the correct way to turn him into a bright spot.

YEAR	TEAM	LVL	AGE	PA	DRC+	VORP	BABIP	BRR	FRAA	WARP
2017	LOU	AAA	25	491	115	22.5	.328	1.0	3B(93): 5.2, 1B(17): -0.3	2.8
2018	LOU	AAA	26	193	164	23.0	.467	2.9	2B(14): -2.3, 1B(14): 0.1	1.7
2018	CIN	MLB	26	124	68	-5.3	.229	-0.5	1B(27): 0.0, RF(17): -1.1	-0.5
2019	TOL	AAA	27	46	27	-5.3	.241	0.5	1B(11): 0.9	-0.2
2019	DET	MLB	27	420	78	-3.3	.336	-0.9	1B(61): -3.7, LF(26): -0.9	-0.7
2020	DET	MLB	28	350	73	-5.3	.314	-0.8	LF 0, 1B -1	-0.6

Brandon Dixon, continued

Batted Ball Distribution

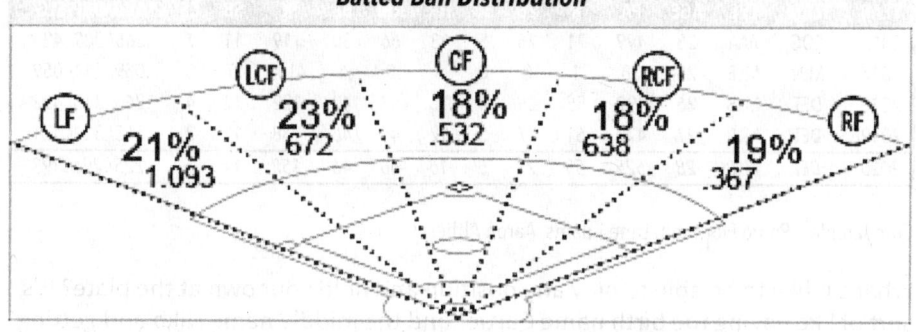

Strike Zone vs LHP   **Strike Zone vs RHP**

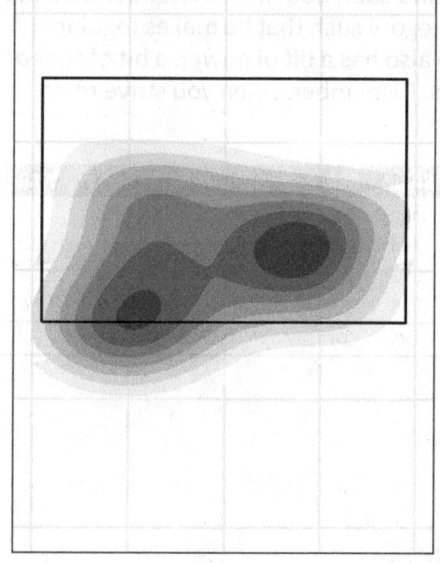
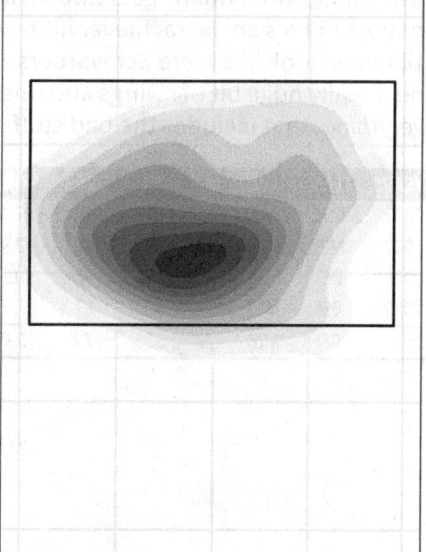

Detroit Tigers 2020

Niko Goodrum UT

Born: 02/28/92   Age: 28   Bats: B   Throws: R
Height: 6'3"   Weight: 218   Origin: Round 2, 2010 Draft (#71 overall)

YEAR	TEAM	LVL	AGE	PA	R	2B	3B	HR	RBI	BB	K	SB	CS	AVG/OBP/SLG
2017	ROC	AAA	25	499	71	25	5	13	66	30	119	11	7	.265/.309/.425
2017	MIN	MLB	25	18	1	0	0	0	0	1	10	0	0	.059/.111/.059
2018	DET	MLB	26	492	55	29	3	16	53	42	132	12	4	.245/.315/.432
2019	DET	MLB	27	472	61	27	5	12	45	46	138	12	3	.248/.322/.421
2020	DET	MLB	28	525	55	22	5	16	60	46	152	14	5	.225/.296/.393

Comparables: Pedro Florimón, Lane Adams, Aaron Altherr

What's it like to be able to play any position and hold your own at the plate? It's sort of like having the birth name Cartier and the middle name Niko and getting to pick which one people call you. Most would trade their childhood blanket for just one of those. The extremely versatile Goodrum was one of five players who started a game last year at every position except pitcher and catcher. He also switch hits. "Utilityman" gets thrown around a lot, both in conversation and the lineup, but he's an overachiever in the category such that he makes regular utilitymen look like mere Schwarbers. He also has a bit of power, a bit of speed and a really huge bit of swings and misses. Remember, when you strive to do *everything*, that includes the bad stuff.

YEAR	TEAM	LVL	AGE	PA	DRC+	VORP	BABIP	BRR	FRAA	WARP
2017	ROC	AAA	25	499	100	17.0	.326	4.4	RF(47): 3.3, 2B(37): -4.2	1.6
2017	MIN	MLB	25	18	48	-2.9	.143	0.2	2B(8): -0.4, RF(1): 0.0	-0.1
2018	DET	MLB	26	492	98	11.9	.312	-1.3	2B(64): 1.0, 1B(37): -0.8	0.9
2019	DET	MLB	27	472	87	7.9	.338	3.4	SS(38): 3.6, 2B(22): -1.9	1.6
2020	DET	MLB	28	525	79	3.9	.295	0.4	SS 8, LF -1	1.2

Niko Goodrum, continued

Batted Ball Distribution

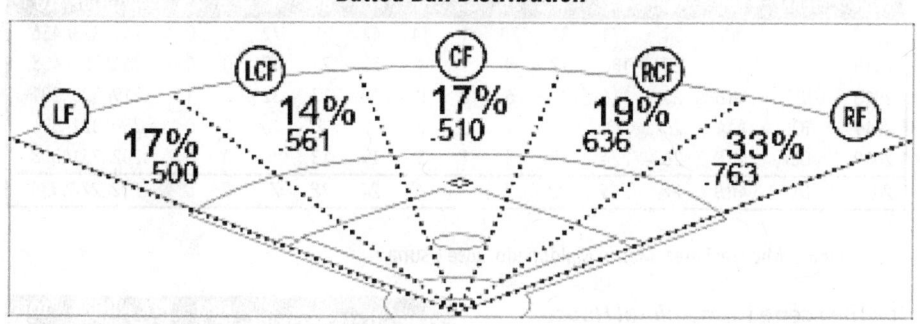

Strike Zone vs LHP

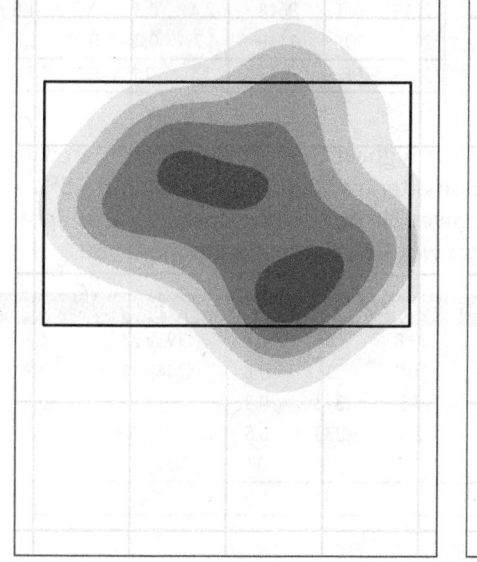

Strike Zone vs RHP

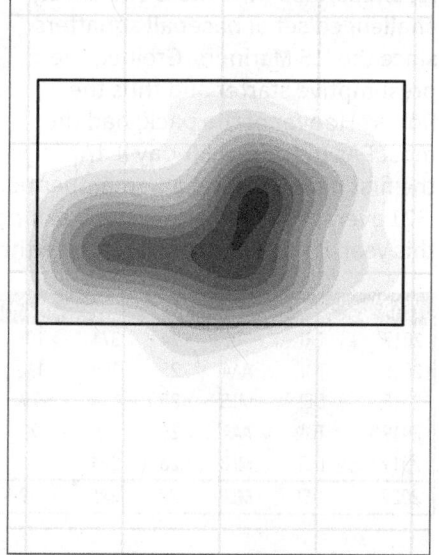

Detroit Tigers 2020

Grayson Greiner C

Born: 10/11/92   Age: 27   Bats: R   Throws: R
Height: 6'6"   Weight: 239   Origin: Round 3, 2014 Draft (#99 overall)

YEAR	TEAM	LVL	AGE	PA	R	2B	3B	HR	RBI	BB	K	SB	CS	AVG/OBP/SLG
2017	ERI	AA	24	371	34	20	1	14	42	38	72	0	0	.241/.323/.436
2018	TOL	AAA	25	180	12	8	1	4	23	21	42	0	0	.266/.350/.405
2018	DET	MLB	25	116	9	6	0	0	12	17	32	0	1	.219/.328/.281
2019	TOL	AAA	26	53	8	1	0	2	4	4	16	0	0	.250/.321/.396
2019	DET	MLB	26	224	18	5	1	5	19	13	70	0	0	.202/.251/.308
2020	DET	MLB	27	245	22	9	1	6	24	18	75	0	0	.212/.277/.336

Comparables: Michael Perez, Martín Maldonado, José Osuna

It's the scene from *Animal House*, except Dean Wormer is just reading off the batting statistics of the 2019 Tigers catchers, who went a combined .176/.226/.300—the most offensively challenged set of baseball squatters since the '15 Mariners. Greiner, the presumptive starter and thus the Robert Hoover of the pack, had the

YEAR	TEAM	P. COUNT	FRM RUNS	BLK RUNS	THRW RUNS	TOT RUNS
2017	ERI	12250	22.4	5.5	0.2	27.3
2018	DET	4428	-0.6	-0.2	0.0	-0.9
2018	TOL	6014	9.5	0.5	0.3	10.0
2019	DET	8618	-2.4	0.3	0.2	-1.8
2019	TOL	1168	1.2	0.0	0.0	1.7
2020	DET	7919	-1.5	-0.1	0.2	-1.4

most PAs (despite a 60-day IL trip) and the highest OBP. While he floundered in the first half, he found a September boon after his back injury in the form of a .321 average, albeit with no walks or power. He otter earn himself a roster spot this year, if not a starting role, but either way he's damn glad to meet you.

YEAR	TEAM	LVL	AGE	PA	DRC+	VORP	BABIP	BRR	FRAA	WARP
2017	ERI	AA	24	371	106	13.8	.266	-3.0	C(93): 27.5	4.6
2018	TOL	AAA	25	180	118	10.9	.336	0.3	C(44): 11.2	2.3
2018	DET	MLB	25	116	79	3.5	.313	0.3	C(30): -0.5	0.3
2019	TOL	AAA	26	53	90	2.0	.333	0.5	C(9): 1.1	0.3
2019	DET	MLB	26	224	56	-1.0	.276	-0.9	C(58): -2.9	-0.5
2020	DET	MLB	27	245	59	-1.8	.291	0.0	C -2	-0.4

Grayson Greiner, continued

Batted Ball Distribution

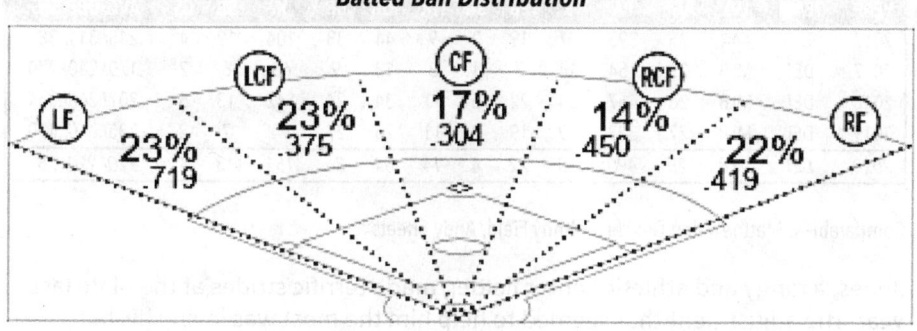

Strike Zone vs LHP   **Strike Zone vs RHP**

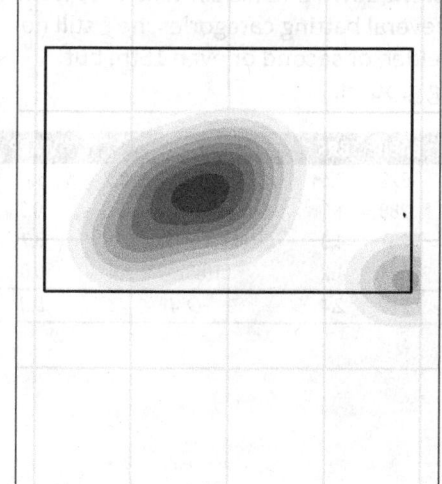
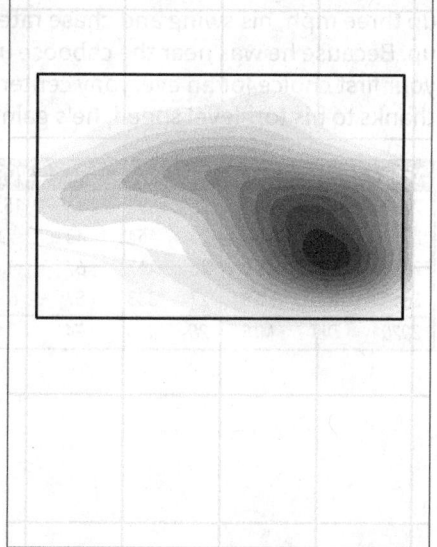

Detroit Tigers 2020

JaCoby Jones CF

Born: 05/10/92   Age: 28   Bats: R   Throws: R
Height: 6'2"   Weight: 201   Origin: Round 3, 2013 Draft (#87 overall)

YEAR	TEAM	LVL	AGE	PA	R	2B	3B	HR	RBI	BB	K	SB	CS	AVG/OBP/SLG
2017	TOL	AAA	25	393	57	19	2	9	44	33	104	12	4	.245/.314/.387
2017	DET	MLB	25	154	14	3	1	3	13	9	65	6	2	.170/.240/.270
2018	DET	MLB	26	467	54	22	6	11	34	24	142	13	5	.207/.266/.364
2019	DET	MLB	27	333	39	19	3	11	26	27	94	7	2	.235/.310/.430
2020	DET	MLB	28	490	50	22	4	14	54	36	151	13	4	.220/.290/.383

Comparables: Matthew den Dekker, Johnny Field, Andy Sheets

Jones, a rangy and athletic center fielder, made terrific strides at the plate last year. The adjustment that seemed to help him the most was laying his bat against his shoulder, as if to calm a previously feral barrel, or store potential energy, or align the chakras or soothe it like an infant who is going through teething (you parents out there know what we're talking about). Whatever the reason, the adjustment showed up in his peripherals: his exit velocity jumped up three mph, his swing and chase rates went down and his contact rates went up. Because he was near the caboose in several batting categories, he's still not your first choice for an everyday center fielder, or second or even 15th, but thanks to his top-level speed, he's gaining ground.

YEAR	TEAM	LVL	AGE	PA	DRC+	VORP	BABIP	BRR	FRAA	WARP
2017	TOL	AAA	25	393	93	15.8	.322	3.6	CF(76): 3.2, LF(7): 0.2	1.6
2017	DET	MLB	25	154	43	-7.9	.288	1.1	CF(51): 2.3, RF(1): 0.0	-0.2
2018	DET	MLB	26	467	67	-1.4	.281	4.3	CF(67): 4.0, LF(55): 2.7	0.7
2019	DET	MLB	27	333	87	6.9	.304	1.2	CF(85): -7.8	0.0
2020	DET	MLB	28	490	74	3.9	.299	2.4	CF 4	0.8

JaCoby Jones, continued

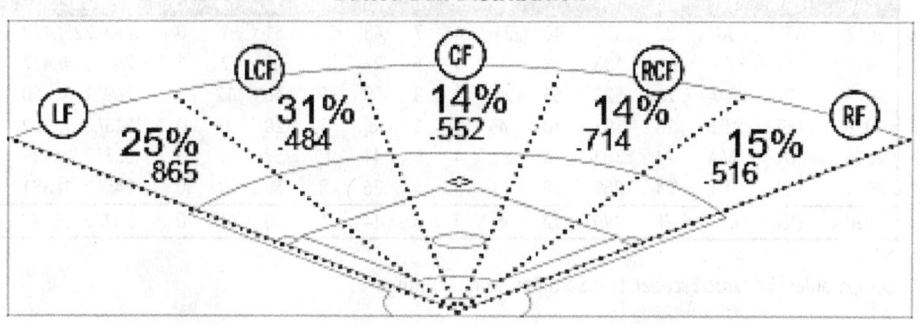

Strike Zone vs LHP   **Strike Zone vs RHP**

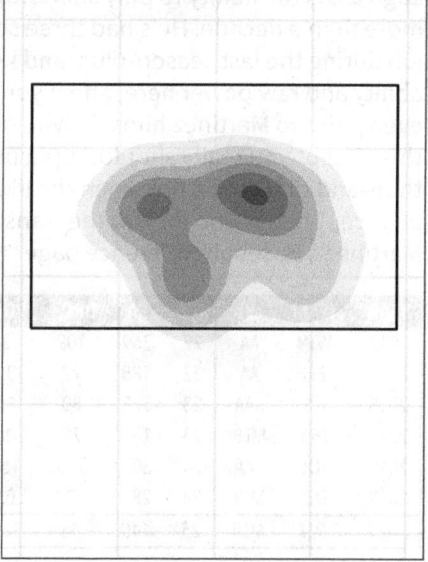

Detroit Tigers 2020

Dawel Lugo 3B
Born: 12/31/94   Age: 25   Bats: R   Throws: R
Height: 6'0"   Weight: 220   Origin: International Free Agent, 2012

YEAR	TEAM	LVL	AGE	PA	R	2B	3B	HR	RBI	BB	K	SB	CS	AVG/OBP/SLG
2017	WTN	AA	22	369	40	21	4	7	43	21	51	1	0	.282/.325/.428
2017	ERI	AA	22	188	18	6	1	6	22	12	21	2	1	.269/.314/.417
2018	TOL	AAA	23	523	56	26	3	3	59	9	66	12	4	.269/.283/.350
2018	DET	MLB	23	101	10	4	1	1	8	7	20	0	0	.213/.267/.309
2019	TOL	AAA	24	303	46	21	4	5	41	15	52	6	3	.333/.370/.489
2019	DET	MLB	24	288	28	11	4	6	26	8	59	0	0	.245/.271/.381
2020	DET	MLB	25	140	12	6	1	3	14	5	30	1	0	.251/.283/.374

Comparables: Eduardo Escobar, Luis Sardiñas, Miguel Andújar

Lugo was traded twice as a prospect for two players who could not possibly be more different: Cliff Pennington and J.D. Martinez. Through parts of two seasons, his career is trending more towards Pennington, with the caveat that Lugo lacks the ability to play shortstop that kept Pennington in the majors for more than a decade. He's had three separate opportunities to stake a claim on a job during the last season-plus, and keeps failing to do so. There's latent hitting ability and raw power here, and if you want to be insanely optimistic you can even point to Martinez himself, who didn't get it going until he was older than this. Except you really shouldn't pin player development hopes on one-in-a-thousand outcomes; not when the likelier outcome is that Lugo is forgotten by all except those who look at the transactions portions of Pennington and/or Martinez's Baseball-Reference page.

YEAR	TEAM	LVL	AGE	PA	DRC+	VORP	BABIP	BRR	FRAA	WARP
2017	WTN	AA	22	369	109	13.7	.310	-1.7	3B(77): 4.5, SS(10): -0.4	2.0
2017	ERI	AA	22	188	97	3.4	.275	-1.5	3B(29): -1.1, 2B(13): 0.6	0.4
2018	TOL	AAA	23	523	80	1.8	.302	-1.1	2B(80): -6.0, 3B(43): -2.0	-0.4
2018	DET	MLB	23	101	77	-1.1	.260	-0.2	2B(27): -3.2	-0.3
2019	TOL	AAA	24	303	119	16.5	.390	-1.0	3B(61): -3.7, 2B(6): 0.9	1.3
2019	DET	MLB	24	288	71	0.2	.288	-0.1	3B(73): -3.7	-0.4
2020	DET	MLB	25	140	68	-2.1	.303	-0.1	3B 0, 2B 0	-0.3

Dawel Lugo, continued

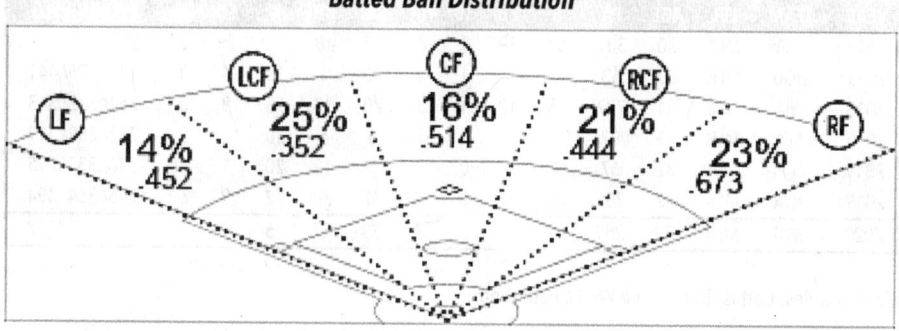

Batted Ball Distribution

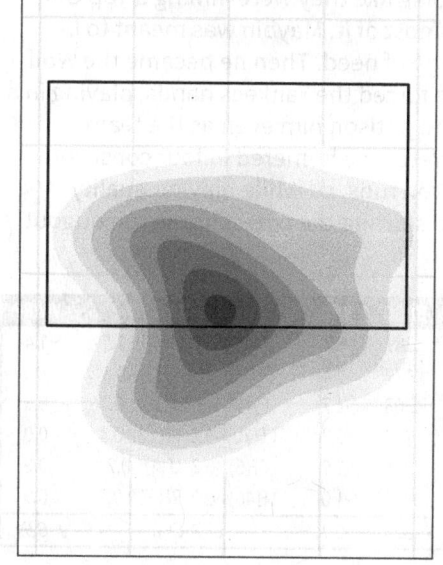

Strike Zone vs LHP

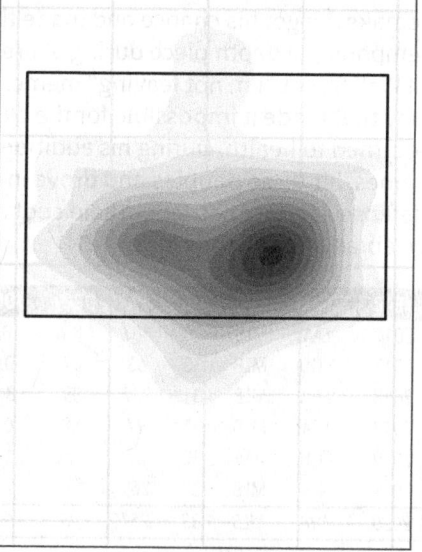

Strike Zone vs RHP

Cameron Maybin OF

Born: 04/04/87 Age: 33 Bats: R Throws: R
Height: 6'3" Weight: 215 Origin: Round 1, 2005 Draft (#10 overall)

YEAR	TEAM	LVL	AGE	PA	R	2B	3B	HR	RBI	BB	K	SB	CS	AVG/OBP/SLG
2017	LAA	MLB	30	387	57	19	1	6	22	48	78	29	5	.235/.333/.351
2017	HOU	MLB	30	63	6	1	1	4	13	3	16	4	3	.186/.226/.441
2018	MIA	MLB	31	287	20	12	1	3	20	32	55	8	5	.251/.338/.343
2018	SEA	MLB	31	97	12	2	1	1	8	6	20	2	0	.242/.289/.319
2019	COH	AAA	32	67	4	3	0	0	5	13	20	1	2	.216/.388/.275
2019	NYA	MLB	32	269	48	17	0	11	32	30	72	9	6	.285/.364/.494
2020	NYA	MLB	33	251	28	11	1	7	28	26	65	9	3	.249/.332/.397

Comparables: Carlos Gómez, Lee Walls, Peter Bourjos

Wham bam thank you Cam was the actual plan when the Yankees acquired Maybin from the Indians. A major leaguer treading water in Triple A for months, he was prepared to fight tooth and nail to stay in the big leagues, if only he had the chance. When Bombers started dropping like they were filming a Top Gun remake, he got his chance and made the most of it. Maybin was meant to be temporary, a depth piece during a dire time of need. Then he became the Wolf of Wall Street "I'm not leaving" meme. He forced the Yankees hands, playing in a way that made it impossible for the club to jettison him even as the team returned to health. During his audition stretch, he homered in four consecutive games, hit three doubles and drove in seven runs, all while playing quality defense at either corner outfield spot and starting the cutest home run dugout celebration of all time. #HugSZN

YEAR	TEAM	LVL	AGE	PA	DRC+	VORP	BABIP	BRR	FRAA	WARP
2017	LAA	MLB	30	387	88	10.0	.289	4.9	LF(45): 2.6, CF(42): 1.5	1.4
2017	HOU	MLB	30	63	87	-0.1	.179	-0.4	CF(15): -0.4, LF(5): -0.3	-0.1
2018	MIA	MLB	31	287	89	8.1	.308	-2.7	LF(44): 2.1, CF(30): -0.7	0.3
2018	SEA	MLB	31	97	88	-0.6	.300	-0.2	CF(20): -1.6, LF(12): 0.4	0.0
2019	COH	AAA	32	67	128	-1.6	.344	-1.9	CF(5): -0.3, LF(4): -0.2	0.2
2019	NYA	MLB	32	269	106	9.1	.365	-1.0	LF(46): -0.5, RF(36): 0.7	0.9
2020	NYA	MLB	33	251	96	6.7	.324	-0.1	LF 2, CF 0	0.9

Cameron Maybin, *continued*

Batted Ball Distribution

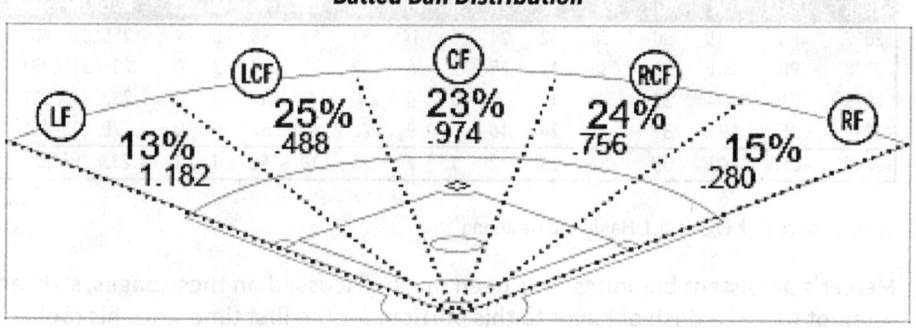

Strike Zone vs LHP

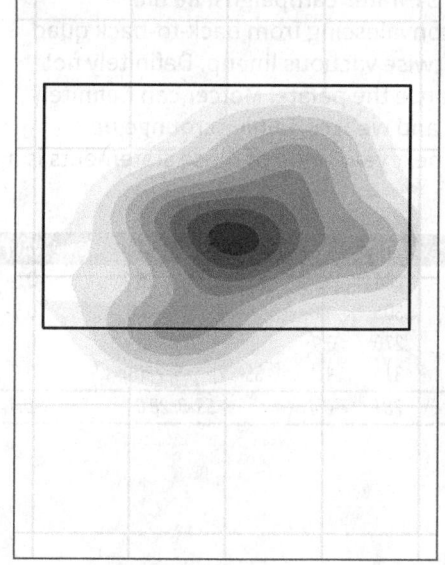

Strike Zone vs RHP

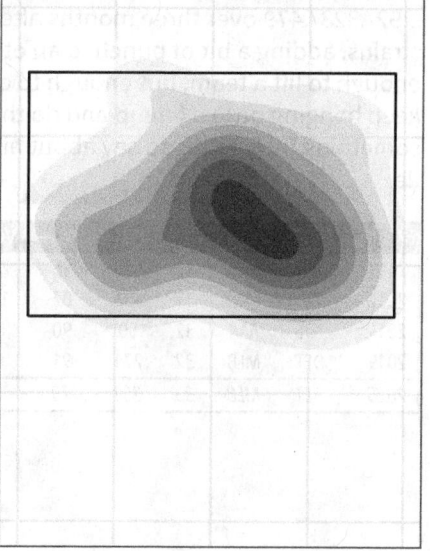

Detroit Tigers 2020

Jordy Mercer SS
Born: 08/27/86 Age: 33 Bats: R Throws: R
Height: 6'3" Weight: 210 Origin: Round 3, 2008 Draft (#79 overall)

YEAR	TEAM	LVL	AGE	PA	R	2B	3B	HR	RBI	BB	K	SB	CS	AVG/OBP/SLG
2017	PIT	MLB	30	558	52	24	5	14	58	51	88	0	4	.255/.326/.406
2018	PIT	MLB	31	436	43	29	2	6	39	32	87	2	0	.251/.315/.381
2019	TOL	AAA	32	50	11	3	0	0	4	5	6	0	0	.233/.340/.302
2019	DET	MLB	32	271	24	16	0	9	22	13	57	0	0	.270/.310/.438
2020	DET	MLB	33	251	23	12	1	5	25	18	52	1	1	.233/.295/.355

Comparables: Zack Cozart, J.J. Hardy, Ian Desmond

Mercer's persistent blandness has been much discussed on these pages, so in an attempt to add a dash of flavor to this portion: for the first time since his rookie season in 2012, he finished a year with more home runs than intentional walks. This was to be expected since he no longer batted eighth for a National League side. (Although he did bat in a 2019 Tigers lineup, so, six of one....) While his seasonal line blended in with much of his Pirates campaigns, he hit .292/.323/.479 over three months after convalescing from back-to-back quad strains, adding a bit of punch to an otherwise vacuous lineup. Definitely not enough to lift a team, but enough to cleanse the palate. Mercer can definitely keep hanging onto a lineup and do this, and we'll certainly scrounge up something interesting to say about him next year—one of these statements is a lie.

YEAR	TEAM	LVL	AGE	PA	DRC+	VORP	BABIP	BRR	FRAA	WARP
2017	PIT	MLB	30	558	96	21.3	.284	-1.2	SS(144): -18.7	0.3
2018	PIT	MLB	31	436	87	10.9	.306	-1.0	SS(117): -3.0	0.9
2019	TOL	AAA	32	50	90	0.9	.270	0.9	SS(7): -0.3	0.1
2019	DET	MLB	32	271	91	8.6	.316	-1.1	SS(59): -0.5, 2B(8): 1.9	0.9
2020	DET	MLB	33	251	73	-1.1	.281	-0.4	SS -3, 2B 0	-0.4

Jordy Mercer, continued

Batted Ball Distribution

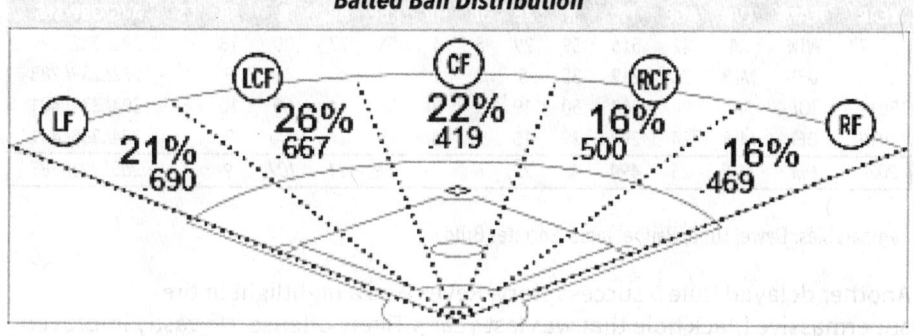

Strike Zone vs LHP   **Strike Zone vs RHP**

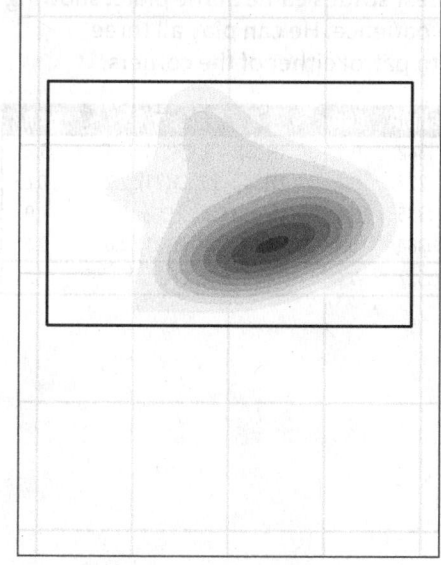
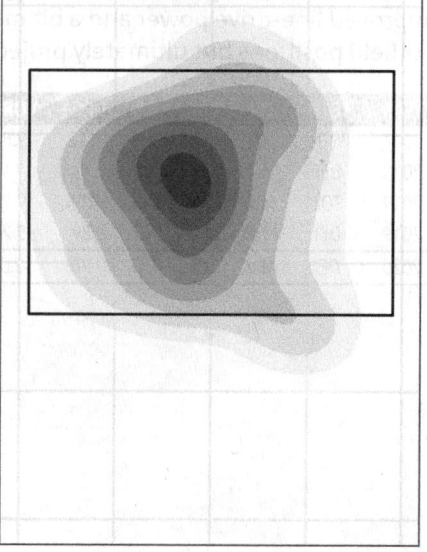

Detroit Tigers 2020

Victor Reyes   OF
Born: 10/05/94   Age: 25   Bats: B   Throws: R
Height: 6'5"   Weight: 215   Origin: International Free Agent, 2011

YEAR	TEAM	LVL	AGE	PA	R	2B	3B	HR	RBI	BB	K	SB	CS	AVG/OBP/SLG
2017	WTN	AA	22	516	59	29	5	4	51	27	80	18	9	.292/.332/.399
2018	DET	MLB	23	219	35	5	3	1	12	5	46	9	1	.222/.239/.288
2019	TOL	AAA	24	308	50	19	1	10	58	14	50	10	6	.304/.334/.481
2019	DET	MLB	24	292	29	16	5	3	25	14	64	9	3	.304/.336/.431
2020	DET	MLB	25	490	43	22	6	7	47	21	107	9	4	.263/.296/.383

Comparables: Dawel Lugo, Raimel Tapia, Sócrates Brito

Another delayed Rule 5 success story, Reyes was a nightlight in the supermassive black hole that was last year's Tigers offense. He vastly improved from an outfielder constantly running into his teammates on fly balls to one who, uh, didn't do that as often. Being able to play against his own kind for a few Triple-A months after being tethered to the 25-player roster due to Rule 5 restrictions certainly helped, too. His greatest strides came at the plate, showing improved line-drive power and a bit more patience. He can play all three outfield positions but ultimately projects to patrol either of the corners.

YEAR	TEAM	LVL	AGE	PA	DRC+	VORP	BABIP	BRR	FRAA	WARP
2017	WTN	AA	22	516	112	9.8	.342	0.1	RF(83): 4.9, CF(57): 10.8	3.7
2018	DET	MLB	23	219	63	-7.9	.277	0.1	LF(34): -3.2, CF(21): 2.2	-0.6
2019	TOL	AAA	24	308	105	9.2	.335	0.4	RF(36): 0.8, CF(31): -0.4	1.0
2019	DET	MLB	24	292	89	5.2	.384	-0.4	CF(37): -0.1, LF(21): 2.0	0.6
2020	DET	MLB	25	490	76	-3.0	.327	-1.0	RF 3, CF 2	0.2

Victor Reyes, continued

Batted Ball Distribution

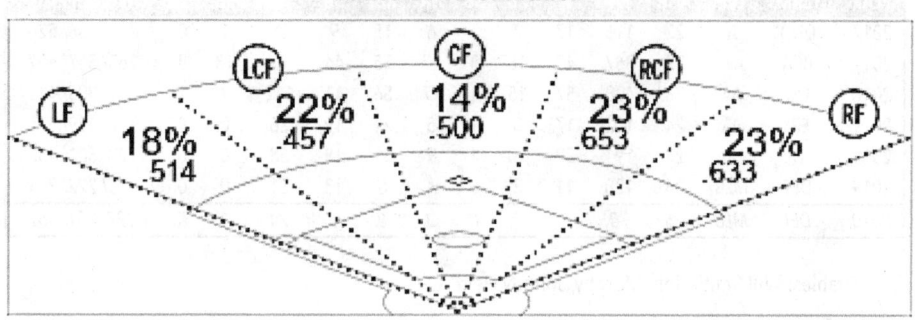

Strike Zone vs LHP

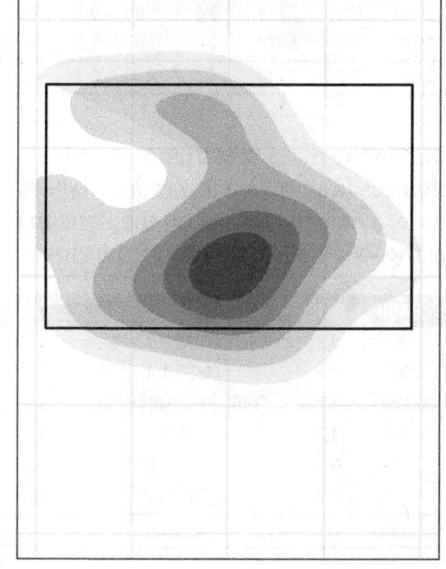

Strike Zone vs RHP

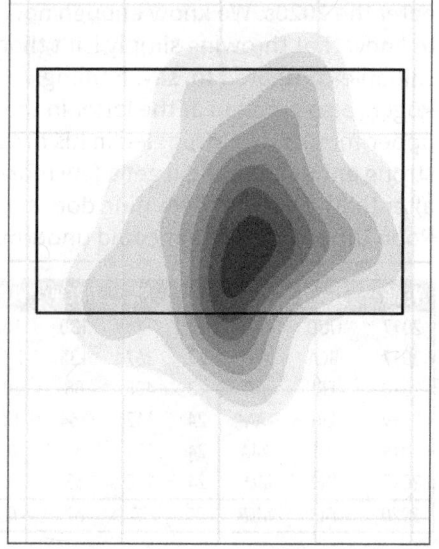

Tigers Player Analysis - 47

Detroit Tigers 2020

Jake Rogers C
Born: 04/18/95   Age: 25   Bats: R   Throws: R
Height: 6'1"   Weight: 205   Origin: Round 3, 2016 Draft (#97 overall)

YEAR	TEAM	LVL	AGE	PA	R	2B	3B	HR	RBI	BB	K	SB	CS	AVG/OBP/SLG
2017	QUD	A	22	116	17	7	1	6	15	9	28	1	0	.255/.336/.520
2017	BCA	A+	22	367	43	18	3	12	55	44	72	13	8	.265/.357/.457
2018	ERI	AA	23	408	57	15	1	17	56	41	112	7	1	.219/.305/.412
2019	ERI	AA	24	112	17	3	1	5	21	19	26	0	0	.302/.429/.535
2019	TOL	AAA	24	191	29	10	1	9	31	18	53	0	0	.223/.321/.458
2019	DET	MLB	24	128	11	3	0	4	8	13	51	0	0	.125/.222/.259
2020	DET	MLB	25	70	7	3	0	2	8	6	24	1	0	.197/.281/.362

Comparables: Will Smith, Tom Murphy, Johnny Field

Rogers is one of the best throwing catchers in the game. That would've been quite exciting in past decades of baseball, and yet seems trivial as we enter the 2020s. We know enough now to know that throwing simply isn't that valuable compared to, say, framing. Rogers also excelled at the latter in the

YEAR	TEAM	P. COUNT	FRM RUNS	BLK RUNS	THRW RUNS	TOT RUNS
2018	ERI	13801	20.3	-0.4	7.2	28.0
2019	DET	5368	-1.4	-2.2	0.2	-3.1
2019	ERI	2716	2.1	0.0	0.7	2.6
2019	TOL	6978	7.3	0.0	1.2	9.0
2020	DET	2740	0.1	-0.4	0.2	-0.2

upper-minors, but struggled in his brief stint in the majors. His reputation is strong enough that he'll get a few more chances (and then a few more chances after that). Even if the framing does translate, a new foe awaits on the horizon in Robo Ump, a threat that could undermine the value of catch-and-throw types.

YEAR	TEAM	LVL	AGE	PA	DRC+	VORP	BABIP	BRR	FRAA	WARP
2017	QUD	A	22	116	130	10.3	.290	0.3	C(21): 0.9	1.0
2017	BCA	A+	22	367	135	29.4	.302	-0.8	C(63): 1.4	2.8
2018	ERI	AA	23	408	88	20.8	.261	2.7	C(98): 29.4, 1B(1): 0.0	4.9
2019	ERI	AA	24	112	164	13.6	.356	-1.7	C(21): 2.3	1.2
2019	TOL	AAA	24	191	88	6.0	.269	-2.7	C(48): 9.5	1.3
2019	DET	MLB	24	128	53	-1.3	.175	-0.4	C(34): -4.0	-0.6
2020	DET	MLB	25	70	67	0.2	.271	-0.1	C 0	0.0

Jake Rogers, continued

Batted Ball Distribution

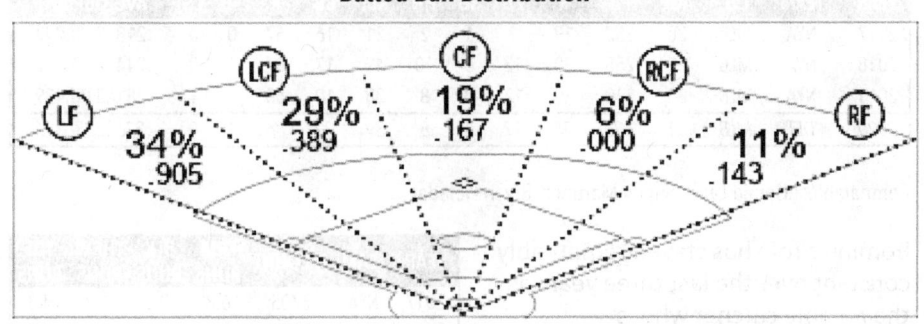

Strike Zone vs LHP   **Strike Zone vs RHP**

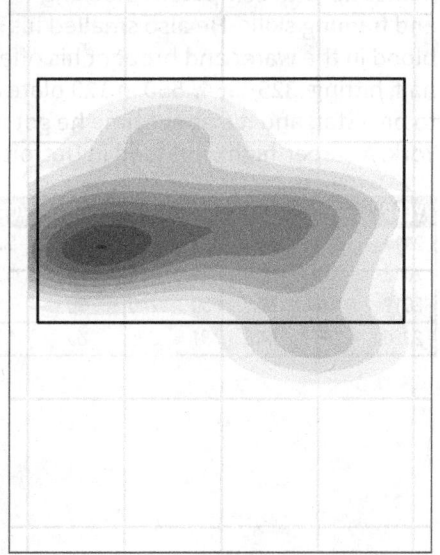

Detroit Tigers 2020

Austin Romine   C
Born: 11/22/88   Age: 31   Bats: R   Throws: R
Height: 6'1"   Weight: 220   Origin: Round 2, 2007 Draft (#94 overall)

YEAR	TEAM	LVL	AGE	PA	R	2B	3B	HR	RBI	BB	K	SB	CS	AVG/OBP/SLG
2017	NYA	MLB	28	252	19	9	1	2	21	16	57	0	0	.218/.272/.293
2018	NYA	MLB	29	265	30	12	0	10	42	17	67	1	0	.244/.295/.417
2019	NYA	MLB	30	240	29	12	0	8	35	10	50	1	1	.281/.310/.439
2020	DET	MLB	31	385	35	17	1	8	39	22	86	1	0	.236/.283/.356

Comparables: Gerald Laird, Sandy Martinez, Bryan Holaday

Romine's role has stayed remarkably constant over the last three years as the reliable catcher who is occasionally forced into short bursts of regular duty. What he lacks in terms of controlling the running game, he makes up with competent blocking and framing skills. He also smelled his impending free agency like a shark smells blood in the water and brought his offensive game to a new level in the second half, hitting .325/.364/.550 in 129 plate appearances. The understudy has longed to be a star, and it's about time he got it, it was just never going to be in New York. A career-high workload in Detroit awaits.

YEAR	TEAM	P. COUNT	FRM RUNS	BLK RUNS	THRW RUNS	TOT RUNS
2017	NYA	8705	6.3	-0.3	-1.3	4.3
2018	NYA	10341	4.2	2.2	0.0	6.3
2019	NYA	9502	-2.2	0.9	0.1	-1.6
2020	DET	17397	0.9	0.8	0.3	2.1

YEAR	TEAM	LVL	AGE	PA	DRC+	VORP	BABIP	BRR	FRAA	WARP
2017	NYA	MLB	28	252	66	-5.2	.277	-1.8	C(67): 4.5, 1B(12): 0.7	0.4
2018	NYA	MLB	29	265	85	4.3	.292	-3.1	C(76): 6.8	1.2
2019	NYA	MLB	30	240	90	9.5	.327	-1.0	C(70): -2.5, P(1): 0.0	0.6
2020	DET	MLB	31	385	65	-1.7	.287	-2.1	C 2	0.1

Austin Romine, continued

Batted Ball Distribution

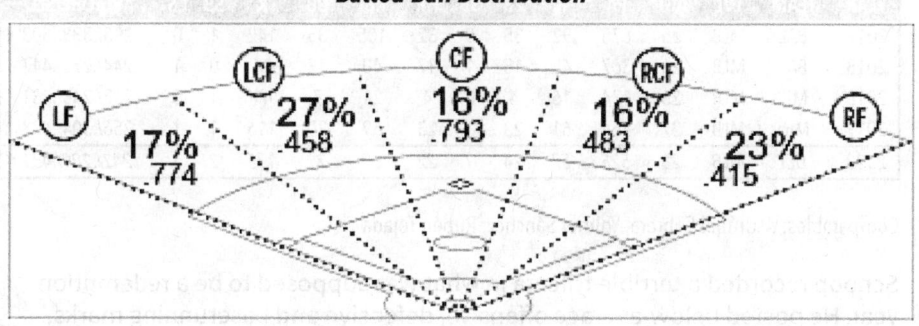

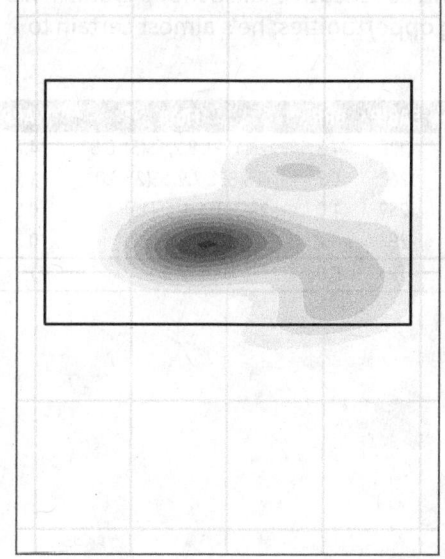

Strike Zone vs LHP

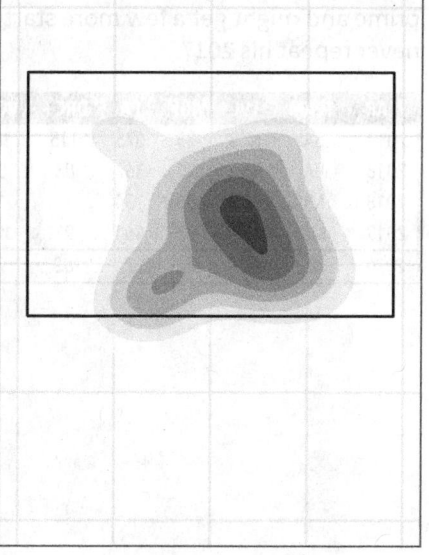

Strike Zone vs RHP

Jonathan Schoop 2B

Born: 10/16/91 Age: 28 Bats: R Throws: R
Height: 6'1" Weight: 225 Origin: International Free Agent, 2008

YEAR	TEAM	LVL	AGE	PA	R	2B	3B	HR	RBI	BB	K	SB	CS	AVG/OBP/SLG
2017	BAL	MLB	25	675	92	35	0	32	105	35	142	1	0	.293/.338/.503
2018	BAL	MLB	26	367	45	18	1	17	40	12	74	0	1	.244/.273/.447
2018	MIL	MLB	26	134	16	4	0	4	21	7	41	1	0	.202/.246/.331
2019	MIN	MLB	27	464	61	23	1	23	59	20	116	1	1	.256/.304/.473
2020	DET	MLB	28	525	57	24	1	22	69	21	135	2	1	.247/.289/.431

Comparables: Asdrúbal Cabrera, Yolmer Sánchez, Rubén Tejada

Schoop recorded a terrible trifecta in what was supposed to be a redemption year. He posted below-average offensive, defensive and baserunning marks, with his new city serving as the backdrop for a frustratingly familiar story. His bat ate garbage-time pitching for lunch, but shrunk consistently in big moments. That, plus his empty slugging profile, left him on the outs by the time the postseason rolled around for a second consecutive fall. Schoop is still in his prime and might get a few more starting opportunities; he's almost certain to never repeat his 2017.

YEAR	TEAM	LVL	AGE	PA	DRC+	VORP	BABIP	BRR	FRAA	WARP
2017	BAL	MLB	25	675	115	38.6	.330	4.2	2B(159): 8.2, SS(5): 0.8	4.7
2018	BAL	MLB	26	367	83	5.4	.262	-0.6	2B(85): 7.9, SS(2): 0.0	1.1
2018	MIL	MLB	26	134	83	-1.0	.259	1.0	2B(31): 1.4, SS(15): 1.1	0.5
2019	MIN	MLB	27	464	93	11.1	.298	-1.8	2B(113): -5.8	0.3
2020	DET	MLB	28	525	82	9.5	.296	0.8	2B 3	1.3

Jonathan Schoop, continued

Batted Ball Distribution

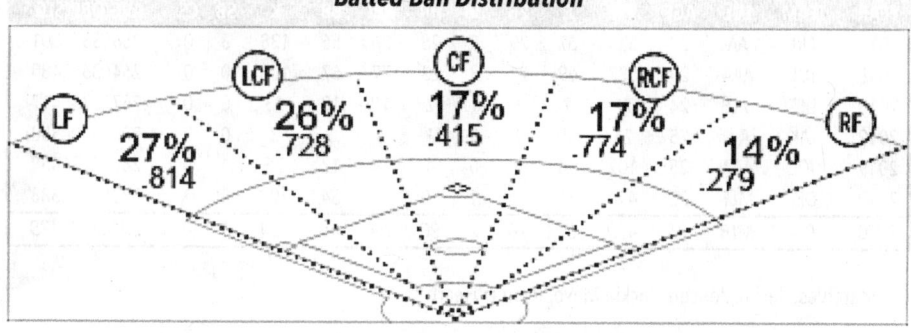

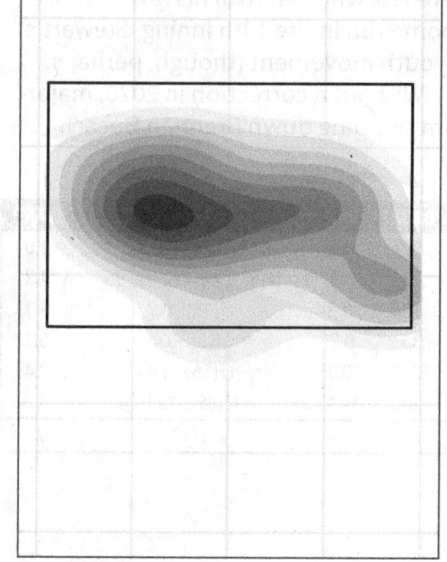
Strike Zone vs LHP

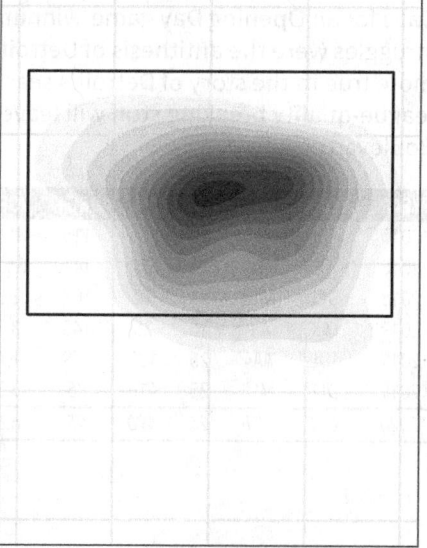
Strike Zone vs RHP

Detroit Tigers 2020

Christin Stewart LF
Born: 12/10/93   Age: 26   Bats: L   Throws: R
Height: 6'0"   Weight: 205   Origin: Round 1, 2015 Draft (#34 overall)

YEAR	TEAM	LVL	AGE	PA	R	2B	3B	HR	RBI	BB	K	SB	CS	AVG/OBP/SLG
2017	ERI	AA	23	555	67	29	3	28	86	56	138	3	0	.256/.335/.501
2018	TOL	AAA	24	522	69	21	3	23	77	67	108	0	0	.264/.364/.480
2018	DET	MLB	24	72	7	1	1	2	10	10	13	0	0	.267/.375/.417
2019	LAK	A+	25	25	2	1	0	1	5	3	3	0	0	.350/.400/.550
2019	TOL	AAA	25	102	14	2	0	4	14	18	25	1	0	.289/.422/.458
2019	DET	MLB	25	416	32	25	1	10	40	34	103	0	1	.233/.305/.388
2020	DET	MLB	26	490	57	20	2	20	64	46	124	1	0	.230/.314/.428

Comparables: Jackie Jensen, Jackie Mayo, Ryan O'Hearn

Quite often there are rookies who don't get the requisite publicity but nonetheless perform well and carry it into the next season. If you're looking for such stories, you're in the wrong paragraph. Stewart was basically gift-wrapped the left field job in 2019 because there were few who can rival his raw power. Save for an Opening Day game-winning home run in the 10th inning, Stewart's struggles were the antithesis of Detroit's youth movement (though, perhaps, more true to the story of Detroit's season). Without a correction in 2020, major-league-quality breaking stuff will leave him skipping down Brennan Boesch Boulevard.

YEAR	TEAM	LVL	AGE	PA	DRC+	VORP	BABIP	BRR	FRAA	WARP
2017	ERI	AA	23	555	115	31.2	.294	-0.8	LF(124): -10.6	1.0
2018	TOL	AAA	24	522	141	36.1	.296	0.8	LF(97): 9.8, RF(12): -0.7	4.3
2018	DET	MLB	24	72	107	3.3	.304	-0.3	LF(15): -0.9	0.1
2019	LAK	A+	25	25	145	3.3	.333	0.2	LF(3): -0.4	0.1
2019	TOL	AAA	25	102	139	7.4	.370	-0.1	LF(16): -3.4	0.4
2019	DET	MLB	25	416	86	3.3	.290	-4.1	LF(89): -12.5	-1.3
2020	DET	MLB	26	490	95	6.6	.273	-2.4	LF -2	0.5

Christin Stewart, continued

Batted Ball Distribution

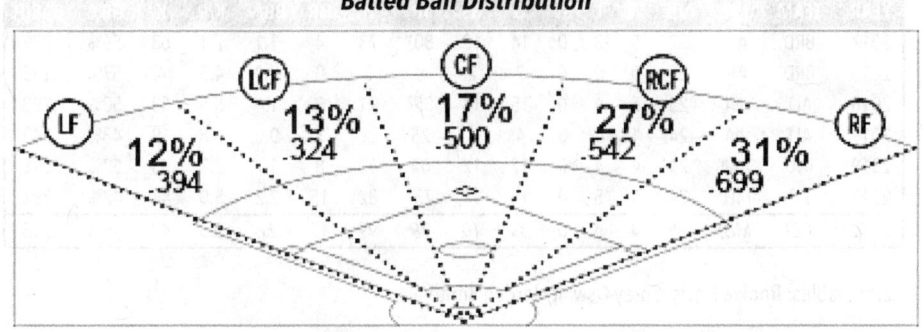

Strike Zone vs LHP   **Strike Zone vs RHP**

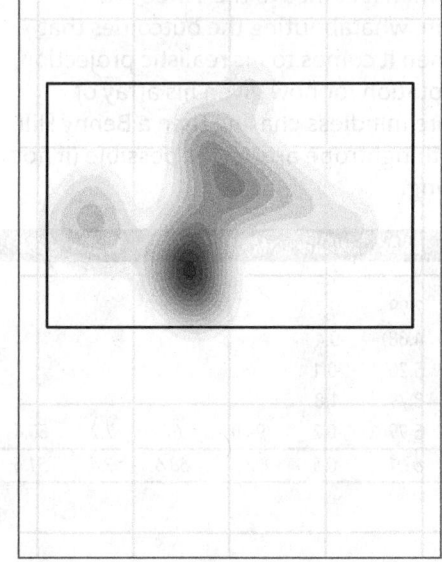
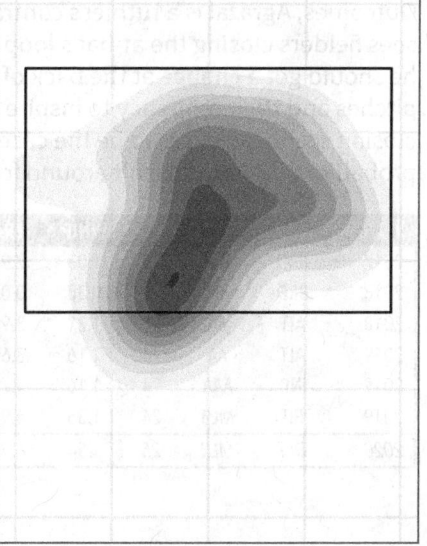

Tigers Player Analysis - 55

Dario Agrazal RHP

Born: 12/28/94 Age: 25 Bats: R Throws: R
Height: 6'2" Weight: 240 Origin: International Free Agent, 2012

YEAR	TEAM	LVL	AGE	W	L	SV	G	GS	IP	H	HR	BB/9	K/9	K	GB%	BABIP
2017	BRD	A+	22	5	3	0	14	13	80^1	73	4	1.1	7.1	63	56%	.289
2018	BRD	A+	23	0	0	0	2	2	8	3	0	0.0	4.5	4	57%	.143
2018	ALT	AA	23	5	6	0	15	14	85^2	91	9	1.4	5.5	52	50%	.298
2019	ALT	AA	24	1	1	0	4	4	25	29	3	0.0	6.8	19	48%	.342
2019	IND	AAA	24	4	4	0	12	12	64	62	8	1.7	7.7	55	52%	.298
2019	PIT	MLB	24	4	5	0	15	14	73^1	82	15	2.2	5.0	41	42%	.283
2020	DET	MLB	25	4	6	0	39	10	79	99	19	2.6	5.3	47	45%	.305

Comparables: Rookie Davis, Corey Oswalt, Jordan Smith

Agrazal is in for a tightrope act. His minor-league résumé is heavy on soft contact and striked outs (not to be confused with strikeouts) and light on balls four. In the majors last year, only one other dude threw more innings with a thinner strikeout rate—Brett Anderson. When it comes to the Three True Outcomes, Agrazal is a ruthless contrarian, whatabouting the outcomes that sees fielders closing the at-bat's loop. When it comes to his realistic projection, he should get a chance at the back of a rotation for now given his array of pitches and their tendency to inspire more mindless chasing than a Benny Hill closing scene. As tends to be the case with tightrope artists, it's possible (if not probable) that Agrazal isn't around for long.

YEAR	TEAM	LVL	AGE	WHIP	ERA	DRA	WARP	MPH	FB%	WHF	CSP
2017	BRD	A+	22	1.03	2.91	3.69	1.5				
2018	BRD	A+	23	0.38	0.00	2.99	0.2				
2018	ALT	AA	23	1.21	3.99	4.88	0.4				
2019	ALT	AA	24	1.16	3.60	5.20	-0.1				
2019	IND	AAA	24	1.16	4.78	3.79	1.8				
2019	PIT	MLB	24	1.36	4.91	5.99	-0.2	93.0	67	7.2	50.4
2020	DET	MLB	25	1.54	6.46	6.01	-0.5	92.7	68.6	7.4	51.6

Dario Agrazal, continued

Pitch Shape vs LHH

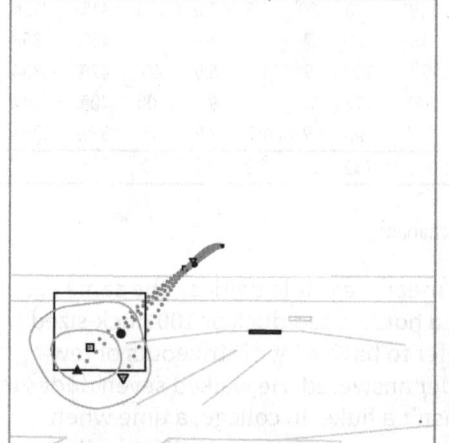

Pitch Shape vs RHH

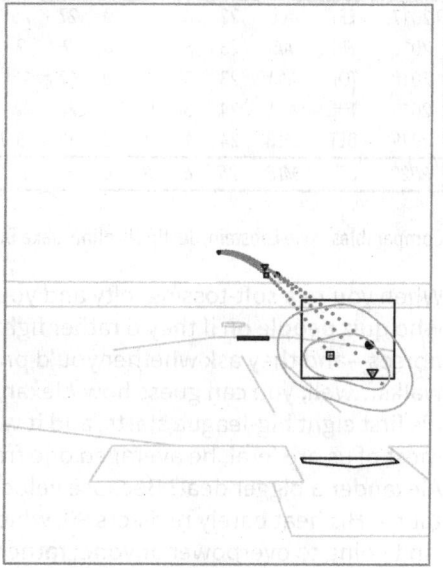

Type	Frequency	Velocity	H Movement	V Movement
● Fastball	12.6%	91 [96]	-8 [95]	-15.5 [101]
☐ Sinker	54.4%	91.2 [93]	-13.7 [93]	-20.5 [100]
+ Cutter				
▲ Changeup	14.1%	85.8 [102]	-12.1 [96]	-24.6 [108]
✕ Splitter				
▽ Slider	18.9%	83 [94]	1.5 [85]	-35.2 [94]
◇ Curveball				
⊕ Slow Curveball				
✱ Knuckleball				
▼ Screwball				

Detroit Tigers 2020

Tyler Alexander   LHP
Born: 07/14/94   Age: 25   Bats: R   Throws: L
Height: 6'2"   Weight: 200   Origin: Round 2, 2015 Draft (#65 overall)

YEAR	TEAM	LVL	AGE	W	L	SV	G	GS	IP	H	HR	BB/9	K/9	K	GB%	BABIP
2017	ERI	AA	22	8	9	0	27	26	138[1]	178	20	1.5	7.8	120	41%	.356
2018	ERI	AA	23	3	2	0	9	9	48	64	7	1.7	6.6	35	45%	.358
2018	TOL	AAA	23	3	6	0	17	15	92	120	9	1.3	5.9	60	47%	.354
2019	TOL	AAA	24	5	10	0	20	16	98[1]	112	18	2.1	9.9	108	40%	.344
2019	DET	MLB	24	1	4	0	13	8	53[2]	68	9	1.2	7.9	47	37%	.347
2020	DET	MLB	25	6	8	0	51	16	116	133	23	2.2	7.0	90	39%	.307

Comparables: Kyle Lobstein, Justin Nicolino, Jake Buchanan

When you're a soft-tossing lefty and you meet the riddle deities—the same set who quiz people on if they'd rather fight a horse-sized duck or 100 duck-sized horses—and they ask whether you'd prefer to have a lot of strikeouts or few walks…well, you can guess how Alexander answered. He walked seven dudes in his first eight big-league starts, and it wasn't a fluke. In college, a time when most of us are feral, he averaged one free pass per nine innings. Why isn't Alexander a bigger deal? Because velocity is the new black, and he is a modest taupe. His heat barely registers 90, which is hardly summer in Texas. Alexander isn't going to overpower anyone; rather, he is going to make his coin by mixing those secondaries like a Sherwin-Williams sales rep taking their job way too seriously. His ceiling is uncomfortably low but the floor is solid steel, and he ought to latch onto the end of a rotation by taking a cue from the gods and asking the batters a riddle of his own: namely, which of his five pitches is next.

YEAR	TEAM	LVL	AGE	WHIP	ERA	DRA	WARP	MPH	FB%	WHF	CSP
2017	ERI	AA	22	1.45	5.07	5.97	-1.4				
2018	ERI	AA	23	1.52	3.75	6.92	-0.9				
2018	TOL	AAA	23	1.45	4.79	6.27	-0.8				
2019	TOL	AAA	24	1.37	5.13	5.40	1.2				
2019	DET	MLB	24	1.40	4.86	5.98	-0.2	92.6	54.6	9.6	51.5
2020	DET	MLB	25	1.39	5.36	5.25	0.3	92.3	55.9	9.8	52.7

Tyler Alexander, continued

Pitch Shape vs LHH

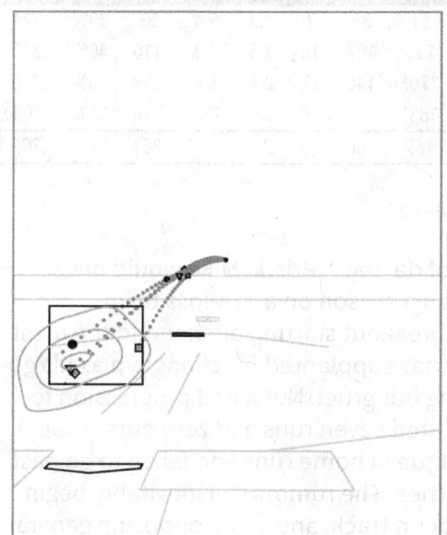

Pitch Shape vs RHH

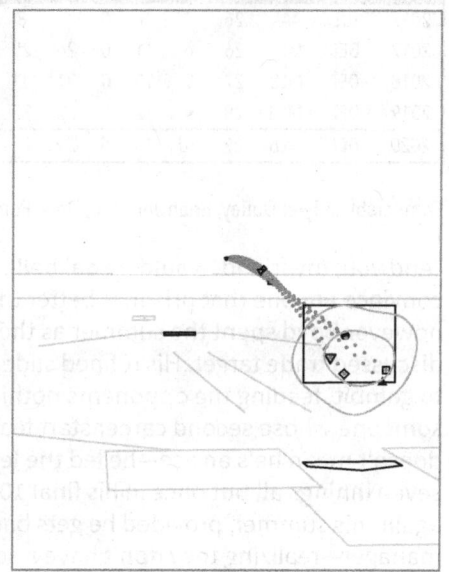

Type	Frequency	Velocity	H Movement	V Movement
● Fastball	29.6%	90.8 [95]	8.2 [94]	-16.2 [99]
☐ Sinker	24.9%	90.8 [91]	13.4 [95]	-19.6 [103]
+ Cutter				
▲ Changeup	11.4%	84.2 [96]	11.6 [98]	-27.9 [99]
✕ Splitter				
▽ Slider	14.9%	85.4 [104]	-2.7 [90]	-28 [115]
◇ Curveball	19.1%	81.3 [109]	-4.2 [87]	-38 [120]
✦ Slow Curveball				
✱ Knuckleball				
▼ Screwball				

Detroit Tigers 2020

Matthew Boyd LHP
Born: 02/02/91   Age: 29   Bats: L   Throws: L
Height: 6'3"   Weight: 234   Origin: Round 6, 2013 Draft (#175 overall)

YEAR	TEAM	LVL	AGE	W	L	SV	G	GS	IP	H	HR	BB/9	K/9	K	GB%	BABIP
2017	TOL	AAA	26	3	3	0	8	8	51	35	7	2.3	9.4	53	39%	.224
2017	DET	MLB	26	6	11	0	26	25	135	157	18	3.5	7.3	110	40%	.330
2018	DET	MLB	27	9	13	0	31	31	170^1	146	27	2.7	8.4	159	30%	.258
2019	DET	MLB	28	9	12	0	32	32	185^1	178	39	2.4	11.6	238	36%	.308
2020	DET	MLB	29	10	10	0	29	29	169	160	30	2.9	10.9	204	34%	.309

Comparables: Tyler Duffey, Brian Johnson, Drew Pomeranz

"And you, my friend, would be da' belle of da' ball." Prison Mike would never convince anyone that prison is better than a season on a 114-loss team, however Boyd spent the summer as the breakout starting pitcher and the most discussed trade target. His refined slider has supplanted his changeup as his go-to gambit, feeding the opponents nothing but gruel. Not a bad progression for someone whose second career start featured seven runs and zero outs. That doesn't mean he's an ace—he led the league in home runs and failed to go past seven innings all but once in his final 10 tries. The rumors will inevitably begin again this summer, provided he gets back on track, and some opposing general manager—realizing they don't have a solid left-handed starter on their potential playoff roster—will be scared straight into a trade.

YEAR	TEAM	LVL	AGE	WHIP	ERA	DRA	WARP	MPH	FB%	WHF	CSP
2017	TOL	AAA	26	0.94	2.82	2.56	1.8				
2017	DET	MLB	26	1.56	5.27	6.46	-1.3	94.6	50.7	11	48
2018	DET	MLB	27	1.16	4.39	5.22	0.2	93.8	48.9	10.9	49
2019	DET	MLB	28	1.23	4.56	3.93	3.7	94.5	53.9	15.6	49.9
2020	DET	MLB	29	1.27	4.23	4.23	2.5	93.6	51.5	13	49.1

Matthew Boyd, continued

Pitch Shape vs LHH	Pitch Shape vs RHH
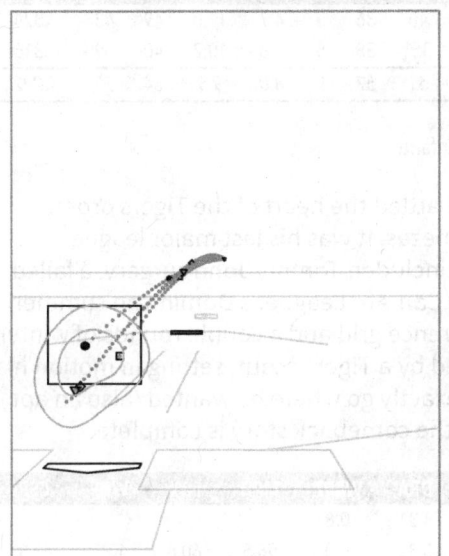	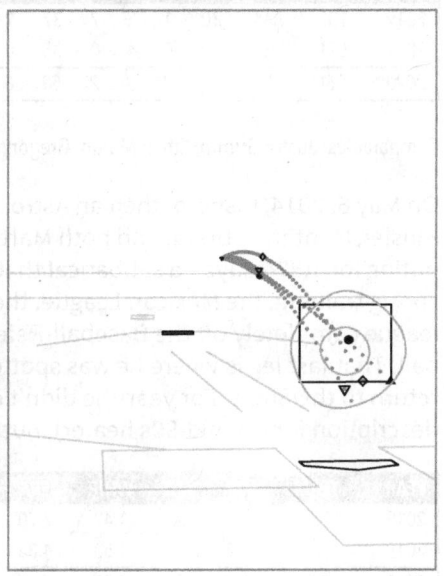

Type	Frequency	Velocity	H Movement	V Movement
● Fastball	50.9%	92.5 [100]	9.2 [90]	-15.6 [101]
☐ Sinker	3.0%	90.2 [87]	13.2 [96]	-21 [98]
+ Cutter				
▲ Changeup	6.0%	79.5 [79]	10.4 [104]	-28.8 [96]
✕ Splitter				
▽ Slider	34.9%	80 [81]	-3.5 [94]	-40.4 [79]
◇ Curveball	5.3%	74.2 [85]	-10.3 [111]	-50.8 [93]
✦ Slow Curveball				
✱ Knuckleball				
▼ Screwball				

Jose Cisnero RHP

Born: 04/11/89 Age: 31 Bats: R Throws: R
Height: 6'3" Weight: 245 Origin: International Free Agent, 2007

YEAR	TEAM	LVL	AGE	W	L	SV	G	GS	IP	H	HR	BB/9	K/9	K	GB%	BABIP
2019	TOL	AAA	30	1	2	7	32	2	40	36	3	4.7	11.0	49	43%	.324
2019	DET	MLB	30	0	4	0	35	0	35^1	35	5	4.8	10.2	40	39%	.316
2020	DET	MLB	31	3	3	2	58	0	61	57	9	4.0	9.5	64	39%	.292

Comparables: Justin Grimm, Ethan Martin, Gregory Infante

On May 6, 2014, Cisnero, then an Astro, battled the heart of the Tigers order: Kinsler, Hunter, Cabrera, and both Martinezes. It was his last major league outing for 1,874 days—a sabbatical that included Tommy John surgery, a failed spring training, the Mexican League, the Can-Am League, a Dominican summer league completely off the Baseball-Reference grid and a couple rounds of winter ball. That last leg is where he was spotted by a Tigers scout, setting in motion his return to the Show. For years he didn't exactly go where he wanted (also an apt description for his mid-90s heater), but the comeback story is complete.

YEAR	TEAM	LVL	AGE	WHIP	ERA	DRA	WARP	MPH	FB%	WHF	CSP
2019	TOL	AAA	30	1.42	2.70	4.31	0.8				
2019	DET	MLB	30	1.53	4.33	5.35	0.0	98.5	60.8	13.5	48.9
2020	DET	MLB	31	1.37	4.44	4.39	0.5	97.6	60.4	13.4	48.6

Jose Cisnero, continued

Pitch Shape vs LHH

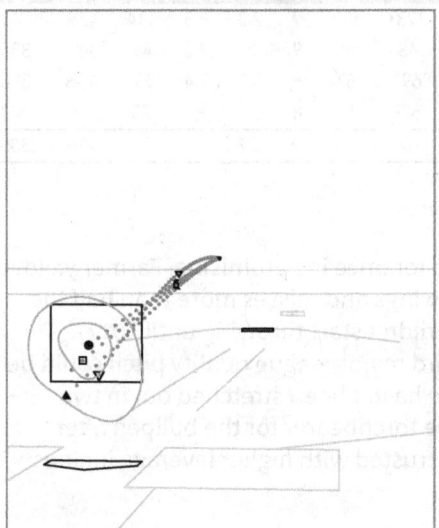

Pitch Shape vs RHH

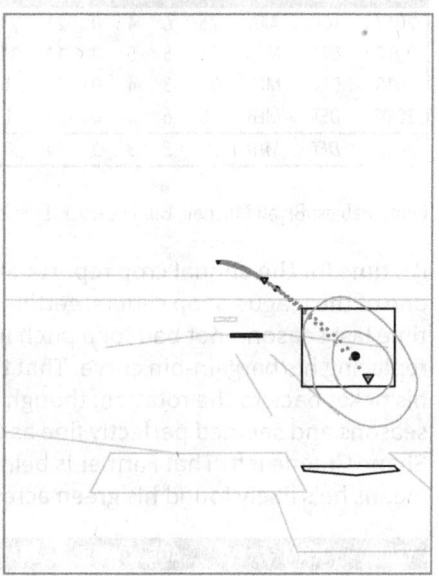

Type	Frequency	Velocity	H Movement	V Movement
● Fastball	50.2%	96.6 [112]	-9.9 [87]	-12.9 [108]
☐ Sinker	10.6%	95.9 [117]	-14 [91]	-18.3 [107]
+ Cutter				
▲ Changeup	8.9%	90.6 [119]	-13.7 [88]	-24.4 [109]
✕ Splitter				
▽ Slider	28.5%	86.9 [111]	4.1 [96]	-30.4 [108]
◇ Curveball				
✦ Slow Curveball				
✱ Knuckleball				
▼ Screwball				

Buck Farmer RHP

Born: 02/20/91 Age: 29 Bats: L Throws: R
Height: 6'4" Weight: 232 Origin: Round 5, 2013 Draft (#156 overall)

YEAR	TEAM	LVL	AGE	W	L	SV	G	GS	IP	H	HR	BB/9	K/9	K	GB%	BABIP
2017	TOL	AAA	26	6	4	0	21	21	123^2	133	9	2.3	8.3	114	43%	.343
2017	DET	MLB	26	5	5	0	11	11	48	55	9	3.8	9.2	49	34%	.336
2018	DET	MLB	27	3	4	0	66	1	69^1	67	6	5.3	7.4	57	41%	.300
2019	DET	MLB	28	6	6	0	73	1	67^2	62	8	3.2	9.7	73	49%	.303
2020	DET	MLB	29	3	3	3	64	0	67	63	9	3.7	9.4	70	45%	.300

Comparables: Bryan Mitchell, Brad Peacock, Erik Johnson

It's time for the annual crop report—and for once it's promising. Farmer yielded one of the league's top sliders, getting swings and misses more than half the time last season—not bad for a pitch he didn't start throwing until 2017, replacing his bargain-bin curve. That third major-league quality pitch could be his ticket back to the rotation, though he hasn't been stretched out in two seasons and seemed perfectly fine as the torchbearer for the bullpen after Shane Greene left. That Farmer is being trusted with higher leverage innings means he's likely found his green acres.

YEAR	TEAM	LVL	AGE	WHIP	ERA	DRA	WARP	MPH	FB%	WHF	CSP
2017	TOL	AAA	26	1.33	3.93	4.48	1.7				
2017	DET	MLB	26	1.56	6.75	5.85	-0.1	94.2	61.2	11.7	45.7
2018	DET	MLB	27	1.56	4.15	5.49	-0.4	96.5	57.6	12	45.3
2019	DET	MLB	28	1.27	3.72	3.92	1.1	96.7	49	13.6	44.3
2020	DET	MLB	29	1.36	4.27	4.23	0.7	95.5	54.6	12.6	45

Buck Farmer, continued

Pitch Shape vs LHH

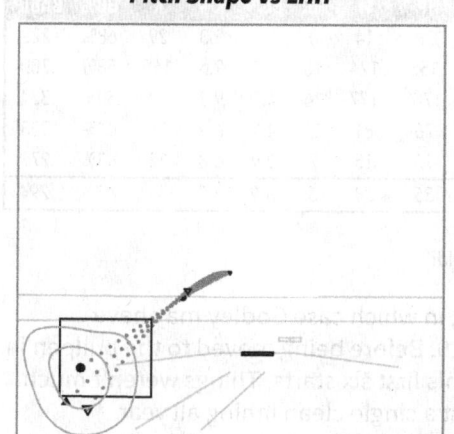

Pitch Shape vs RHH

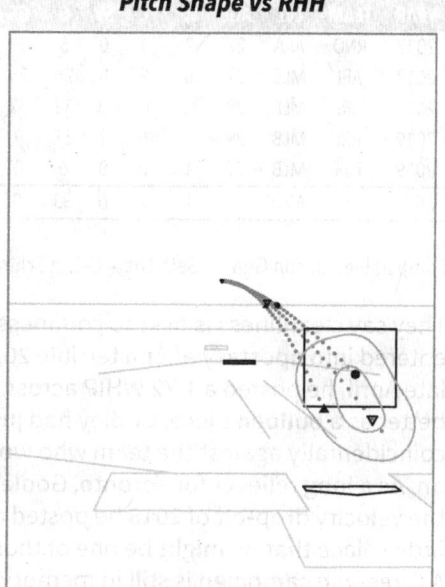

Type	Frequency	Velocity	H Movement	V Movement
● Fastball	48.8%	95.3 [108]	-10.3 [85]	-12.9 [108]
☐ Sinker				
+ Cutter				
▲ Changeup	26.0%	88.4 [111]	-13.6 [88]	-29.3 [94]
✕ Splitter				
▽ Slider	25.0%	82.7 [93]	1.7 [86]	-33.2 [100]
◇ Curveball				
✦ Slow Curveball				
✱ Knuckleball				
▼ Screwball				

Zack Godley RHP

Born: 04/21/90   Age: 30   Bats: R   Throws: R
Height: 6'3"   Weight: 240   Origin: Round 10, 2013 Draft (#288 overall)

YEAR	TEAM	LVL	AGE	W	L	SV	G	GS	IP	H	HR	BB/9	K/9	K	GB%	BABIP
2017	RNO	AAA	27	2	1	0	5	3	28	14	0	5.5	9.3	29	68%	.222
2017	ARI	MLB	27	8	9	0	26	25	155	124	15	3.1	9.6	165	58%	.280
2018	ARI	MLB	28	15	11	0	33	32	178[1]	177	16	4.1	9.3	185	50%	.324
2019	ARI	MLB	29	3	5	2	27	9	76	81	12	4.1	6.9	58	44%	.303
2019	TOR	MLB	29	1	0	0	6	0	16	15	2	3.9	6.8	12	43%	.277
2020	DET	MLB	30	2	2	0	33	0	35	34	5	3.9	8.0	31	47%	.294

Comparables: Justin Grimm, Seth Lugo, Calvin Schiraldi

They say cleanliness is next to godliness, in which case Godley may have entered into apostasy after a terrible 2019. Before being moved to the bullpen in late April, he posted a 1.72 WHIP across his first six starts. Things weren't much better as a bullpen piece; Godley had just a single clean inning all year, coincidentally against the team who would take him when the D-backs moved on. As a long reliever for Toronto, Godley was tolerable, but even after arresting the velocity drop-off of 2018 he posted a career-worst strikeout rate, providing little solace that he might be one of those starters enlivened by a move to relief. A three-win campaign is still in memory, though, giving reason to hope he might return to grace in his age-30 season.

YEAR	TEAM	LVL	AGE	WHIP	ERA	DRA	WARP	MPH	FB%	WHF	CSP
2017	RNO	AAA	27	1.11	2.57	1.97	1.1				
2017	ARI	MLB	27	1.14	3.37	3.69	3.3	93.3	56.9	13.7	42.3
2018	ARI	MLB	28	1.45	4.74	4.78	1.1	92.0	54.4	12.2	43.4
2019	ARI	MLB	29	1.53	6.39	6.70	-1.0	91.8	65.3	11.1	44.8
2019	TOR	MLB	29	1.38	3.94	5.26	0.0	91.6	65.3	12.4	39.5
2020	DET	MLB	30	1.42	4.70	4.70	0.2	91.6	58	12.3	43.2

Zack Godley, continued

Pitch Shape vs LHH

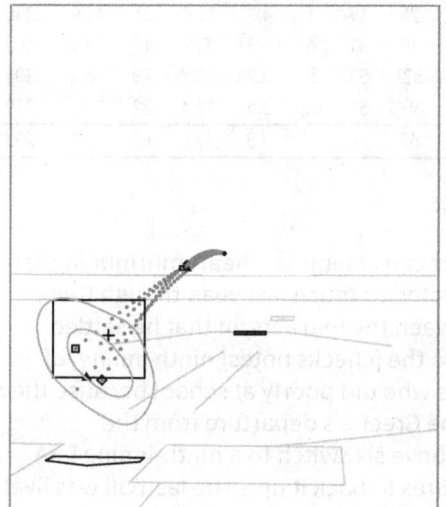

Pitch Shape vs RHH

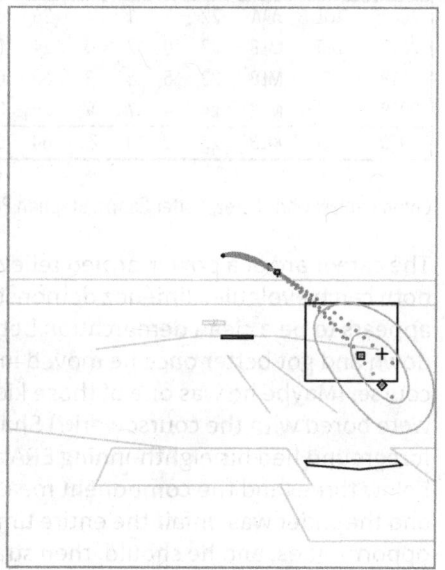

Type	Frequency	Velocity	H Movement	V Movement
● Fastball				
☐ Sinker	34.6%	90.2 [87]	-12 [104]	-25.7 [81]
+ Cutter	17.2%	88.8 [101]	-0.8 [85]	-24.2 [99]
▲ Changeup	6.1%	83.5 [94]	-9.7 [107]	-33.7 [82]
✕ Splitter				
▽ Slider				
◇ Curveball	42.1%	82 [111]	2.4 [79]	-42.3 [111]
✦ Slow Curveball				
✱ Knuckleball				
▼ Screwball				

Detroit Tigers 2020

Joe Jiménez   RHP
Born: 01/17/95   Age: 25   Bats: R   Throws: R
Height: 6'3"   Weight: 272   Origin: Undrafted Free Agent, 2013

YEAR	TEAM	LVL	AGE	W	L	SV	G	GS	IP	H	HR	BB/9	K/9	K	GB%	BABIP
2017	TOL	AAA	22	1	1	4	26	0	25	19	1	4.3	13.0	36	43%	.340
2017	DET	MLB	22	0	2	0	24	0	19	31	4	4.3	8.1	17	37%	.403
2018	DET	MLB	23	5	4	3	68	0	62^2	53	5	3.2	11.2	78	36%	.304
2019	DET	MLB	24	4	7	9	66	0	59^2	56	13	3.5	12.4	82	30%	.319
2020	DET	MLB	25	3	3	26	64	0	67	56	10	3.3	11.6	86	32%	.293

Comparables: Chris Perez, Carter Capps, Stephen Pryor

The career arc of a power-armed reliever can resemble a heart murmur in that both can be volatile. Jiménez demonstrated as much last year, though there appears to be a clean demarcation between the two acts, in that he settled down and got better once he moved into the [checks notes] ninth inning, of course. (Maybe he was one of those kids who did poorly at school because they were bored with the coursework?) Shane Greene's departure from the foreground had his eighth-inning ERA above six switch to a ninth-inning ERA below three (and the component measures to back it up). The fastball was lively and the slider was unfair the entire time. If he gets more ninth inning opportunities, and he should, then strap in. It will probably work out. Probably.

YEAR	TEAM	LVL	AGE	WHIP	ERA	DRA	WARP	MPH	FB%	WHF	CSP
2017	TOL	AAA	22	1.24	1.44	2.78	0.7				
2017	DET	MLB	22	2.11	12.32	5.25	0.0	97.8	63.1	12.8	52
2018	DET	MLB	23	1.20	4.31	3.05	1.4	97.9	67.2	14.9	47.3
2019	DET	MLB	24	1.32	4.37	4.01	0.9	97.4	68.3	15.7	51.4
2020	DET	MLB	25	1.20	3.64	3.73	1.1	97.4	68.9	15.3	51.4

Joe Jiménez, continued

Pitch Shape vs LHH

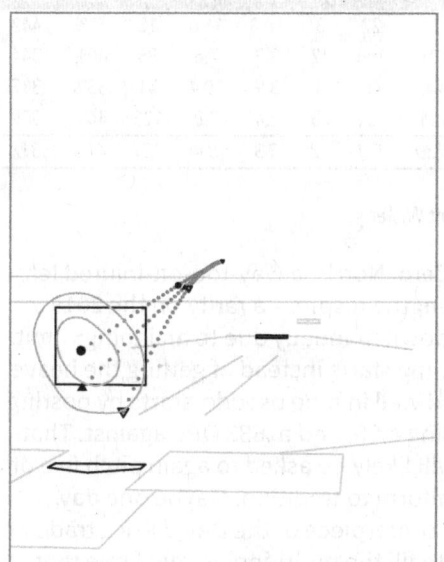

Pitch Shape vs RHH

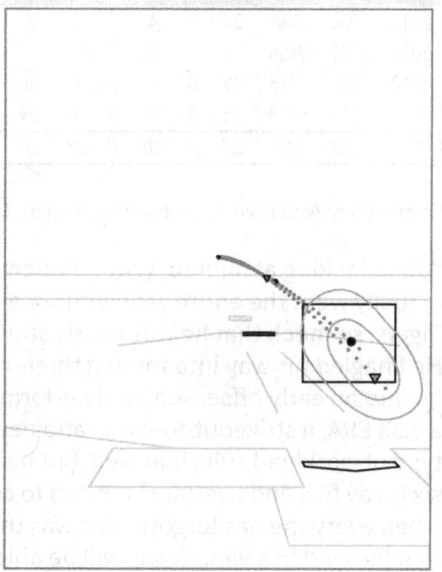

Type	Frequency	Velocity	H Movement	V Movement
● Fastball	68.3%	95.6 [109]	-9.5 [88]	-11.4 [112]
□ Sinker				
+ Cutter				
▲ Changeup	5.8%	89.6 [116]	-14.8 [83]	-24.9 [107]
✕ Splitter				
▽ Slider	25.9%	86.5 [109]	5 [100]	-29.2 [111]
◇ Curveball				
⊕ Slow Curveball				
✱ Knuckleball				
▼ Screwball				

Detroit Tigers 2020

Daniel Norris LHP

Born: 04/25/93 Age: 27 Bats: L Throws: L
Height: 6'2" Weight: 185 Origin: Round 2, 2011 Draft (#74 overall)

YEAR	TEAM	LVL	AGE	W	L	SV	G	GS	IP	H	HR	BB/9	K/9	K	GB%	BABIP
2017	TOL	AAA	24	0	4	0	6	6	14	22	3	10.3	11.6	18	50%	.442
2017	DET	MLB	24	5	8	0	22	18	101^2	120	12	3.9	7.6	86	40%	.344
2018	DET	MLB	25	0	5	0	11	8	44^1	46	8	3.9	10.4	51	33%	.317
2019	DET	MLB	26	3	13	0	32	29	144^1	154	25	2.4	7.8	125	44%	.309
2020	DET	MLB	27	7	10	0	26	26	130	141	22	3.3	8.4	121	41%	.317

Comparables: Aaron Sanchez, Eduardo Rodriguez, Matt Wisler

You're looking at Injured Starter Patient Zero. Norris, a way-too-oft-injured lefty, actually went the entire year without a lengthy respite—a rarity on the 2019 Tigers, so much that he was nearly shut down manually due to an innings limit. He finagled his way into tossing three-inning starts instead of getting the heave ho into an early offseason, and performed well in nine pseudo-starts by posting a 3.33 ERA, a strikeout-to-walk ratio nearing 4.00, and a .683 OPS against. That type of workload suits him well, but he will likely be asked to again pitch five or six (okay five and five-plus) innings to conform to tradition. Maybe one day, when everyone has forgotten he was the centerpiece of the David Price trade or that he lived in a van, Norris will be able to fill the multi-inning relief role that seems to suit him best. Just make sure you check the rest of the relievers for symptoms regularly.

YEAR	TEAM	LVL	AGE	WHIP	ERA	DRA	WARP	MPH	FB%	WHF	CSP
2017	TOL	AAA	24	2.71	12.21	9.01	-0.5				
2017	DET	MLB	24	1.61	5.31	6.48	-1.1	95.5	55	10	45.1
2018	DET	MLB	25	1.47	5.68	5.12	0.1	92.5	52.7	11.4	49.4
2019	DET	MLB	26	1.33	4.49	5.18	0.9	93.1	51.6	10.9	50.1
2020	DET	MLB	27	1.45	5.15	4.97	0.9	93.2	53.3	10.9	49.2

Daniel Norris, continued

Pitch Shape vs LHH

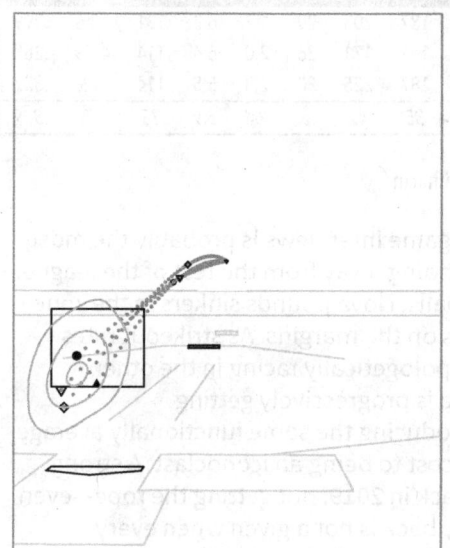

Pitch Shape vs RHH

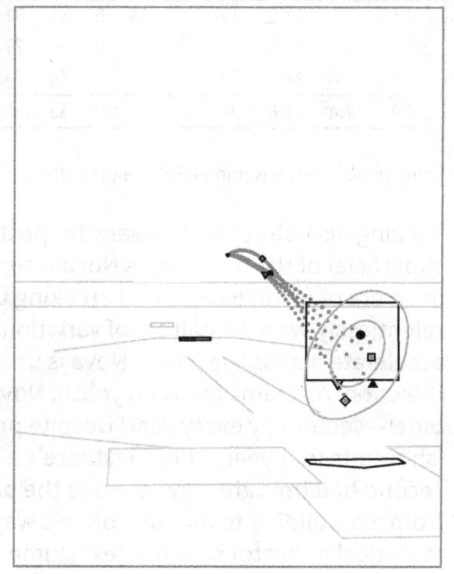

Type	Frequency	Velocity	H Movement	V Movement
● Fastball	45.1%	91.1 [96]	6 [104]	-15.1 [102]
☐ Sinker	6.4%	90.8 [91]	12.7 [100]	-20.6 [99]
+ Cutter				
▲ Changeup	19.2%	86 [103]	10.7 [102]	-33.2 [83]
✕ Splitter				
▽ Slider	22.7%	84.6 [101]	-4.3 [97]	-33.3 [99]
◇ Curveball	6.5%	76.2 [92]	-6.2 [95]	-55.6 [83]
⊕ Slow Curveball				
✻ Knuckleball				
▼ Screwball				

Detroit Tigers 2020

Iván Nova RHP

Born: 01/12/87 Age: 33 Bats: R Throws: R
Height: 6'5" Weight: 250 Origin: International Free Agent, 2004

YEAR	TEAM	LVL	AGE	W	L	SV	G	GS	IP	H	HR	BB/9	K/9	K	GB%	BABIP
2017	PIT	MLB	30	11	14	0	31	31	187	203	29	1.7	6.3	131	48%	.299
2018	PIT	MLB	31	9	9	0	29	29	161	171	26	2.0	6.4	114	47%	.288
2019	CHA	MLB	32	11	12	0	34	34	187	225	30	2.3	5.5	114	47%	.322
2020	CHA	MLB	33	2	2	0	33	0	35	42	6	2.4	5.9	23	47%	.309

Comparables: Jason Hammel, Pat Hentgen, Jhoulys Chacín

Tucking his t-shirt into his jeans for postgame interviews is probably the most superficial of the many ways Nova is trending away from the rest of the league. In an era of fastball carry and breaking balls, Nova pounds sinkers in the zone relentlessly with a small set of variations on the margins. As strikeout rates accelerate across the game, Nova is unapologetically racing in the other direction. As teams focus on youth, Nova is progressively getting older—seemingly every year! Despite producing the same functionally average-ish results four years-running, there's a cost to being an iconoclast. A strong second half brought Nova even to the pack in 2019, but getting the rope—even from a rebuilding team—to work his way back is not a given when every statistical indicator says his next slump is just as likely to be the end of the line as it is to be the standard rough patch that his contact-heavy approach invites.

YEAR	TEAM	LVL	AGE	WHIP	ERA	DRA	WARP	MPH	FB%	WHF	CSP
2017	PIT	MLB	30	1.28	4.14	4.71	1.8	95.1	68.1	9	49.5
2018	PIT	MLB	31	1.28	4.19	4.60	1.3	95.3	66.9	9.7	46.6
2019	CHA	MLB	32	1.45	4.72	7.54	-3.6	94.6	54.2	9	47
2020	CHA	MLB	33	1.46	5.45	5.46	-0.1	93.9	60.7	9.1	46.9

Iván Nova, continued

Pitch Shape vs LHH
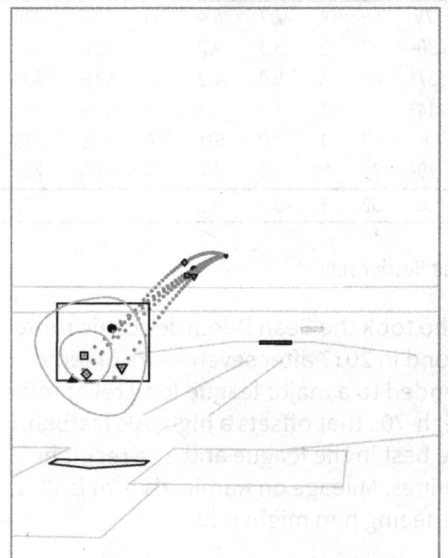

Pitch Shape vs RHH
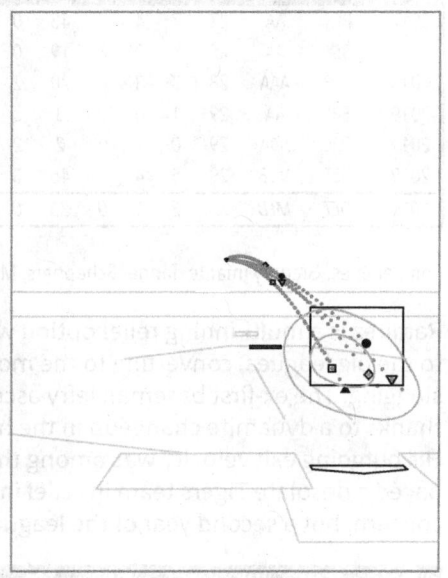

Type	Frequency	Velocity	H Movement	V Movement
● Fastball	15.6%	92.9 [101]	-10.2 [85]	-18 [95]
□ Sinker	38.6%	92.6 [100]	-14.5 [88]	-22.2 [94]
+ Cutter				
▲ Changeup	16.1%	86.5 [105]	-14.1 [86]	-26.4 [103]
× Splitter				
▽ Slider	12.9%	87 [111]	-2.6 [68]	-25.2 [123]
◇ Curveball	16.8%	80.1 [105]	2.9 [81]	-43.5 [109]
✧ Slow Curveball				
✳ Knuckleball				
▼ Screwball				

Detroit Tigers 2020

Nick Ramirez   LHP
Born: 08/01/89   Age: 30   Bats: L   Throws: L
Height: 6'3"   Weight: 240   Origin: Round 4, 2011 Draft (#131 overall)

YEAR	TEAM	LVL	AGE	W	L	SV	G	GS	IP	H	HR	BB/9	K/9	K	GB%	BABIP
2017	BLX	AA	27	7	4	3	48	0	79	56	4	2.7	6.4	56	49%	.230
2018	BLX	AA	28	8	0	1	19	0	30^2	17	2	3.8	9.7	33	55%	.205
2018	CSP	AAA	28	3	3	0	20	2	37^2	44	3	5.0	4.3	18	52%	.308
2019	ERI	AA	29	1	0	0	3	3	14^1	11	1	1.3	12.6	20	55%	.312
2019	TOL	AAA	29	0	1	0	2	2	9	12	1	3.0	10.0	10	45%	.393
2019	DET	MLB	29	5	4	0	46	0	79^2	76	11	4.0	8.4	74	47%	.286
2020	DET	MLB	30	2	2	0	33	0	35	32	5	3.7	8.2	32	47%	.277

Comparables: Gregory Infante, Tanner Scheppers, Matt Buschmann

Ramirez is a multi-inning relief option who took the Sean Doolittle scenic route to the big leagues, converting to the mound in 2017 after seven years of tepid slugging. The ex-first baseman lefty ascended to a major league long relief role thanks to a dynamite changeup in the high-70s that offsets a high-80s fastball. His outgoing exit velocity was among the best in the league and as a result he paced a desolate Tigers team in relief innings. Mileage on Ramirez's arm isn't a concern, but a second year of the league seeing him might be.

YEAR	TEAM	LVL	AGE	WHIP	ERA	DRA	WARP	MPH	FB%	WHF	CSP
2017	BLX	AA	27	1.01	1.37	3.26	1.4				
2018	BLX	AA	28	0.98	1.76	2.97	0.7				
2018	CSP	AAA	28	1.73	5.73	5.87	-0.3				
2019	ERI	AA	29	0.91	2.51	2.98	0.3				
2019	TOL	AAA	29	1.67	2.00	5.17	0.1				
2019	DET	MLB	29	1.39	4.07	4.52	0.7	91.6	30.1	13.2	41.2
2020	DET	MLB	30	1.32	4.08	4.26	0.4	90.9	30	13.2	41.1

Nick Ramirez, continued

Pitch Shape vs LHH

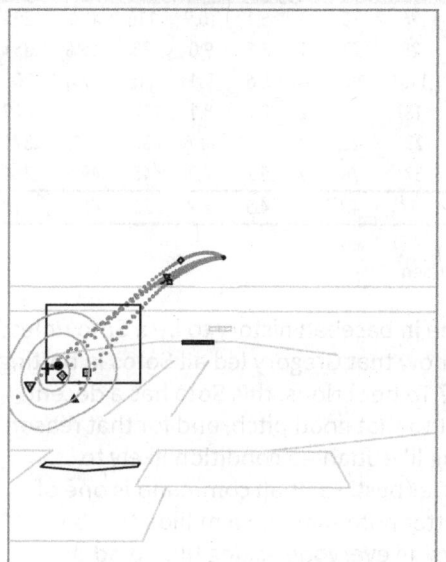

Pitch Shape vs RHH

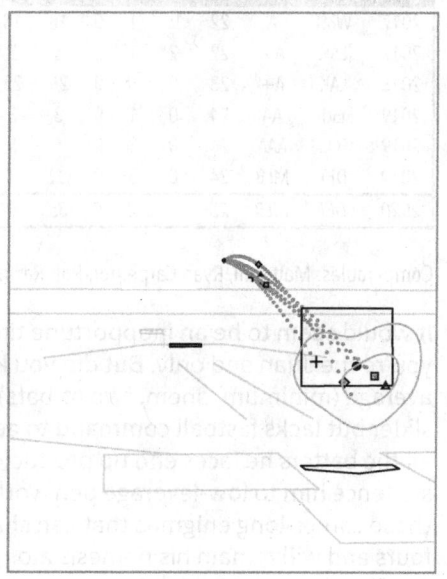

Type	Frequency	Velocity	H Movement	V Movement
● Fastball	15.3%	90.4 [94]	10.7 [83]	-17.7 [95]
☐ Sinker	14.8%	89.4 [83]	13.1 [97]	-22.1 [94]
+ Cutter	28.4%	87.3 [92]	1.4 [81]	-24.3 [99]
▲ Changeup	32.0%	79.3 [79]	11.6 [98]	-31.5 [88]
✕ Splitter				
▽ Slider	3.7%	83.9 [98]	-2.1 [88]	-30.9 [106]
◇ Curveball	5.7%	78.6 [100]	-2.4 [79]	-47.6 [100]
⊕ Slow Curveball				
✳ Knuckleball				
▼ Screwball				

Gregory Soto LHP

Born: 02/11/95 Age: 25 Bats: L Throws: L
Height: 6'1" Weight: 240 Origin: International Free Agent, 2012

YEAR	TEAM	LVL	AGE	W	L	SV	G	GS	IP	H	HR	BB/9	K/9	K	GB%	BABIP
2017	WMI	A	22	10	1	0	18	18	96	70	3	5.1	10.9	116	45%	.295
2017	LAK	A+	22	2	1	0	5	5	28	27	1	3.5	9.0	28	56%	.351
2018	LAK	A+	23	8	8	0	25	23	113^1	101	4	5.6	9.1	115	47%	.306
2019	ERI	AA	24	0	1	0	3	3	13^1	10	2	2.7	8.1	12	54%	.229
2019	TOL	AAA	24	0	3	0	6	5	23^1	25	2	5.0	11.6	30	48%	.371
2019	DET	MLB	24	0	5	0	33	7	57^2	74	9	5.2	7.0	45	49%	.344
2020	DET	MLB	25	2	2	0	35	0	37	42	6	4.5	6.9	28	48%	.318

Comparables: Matt Hall, Ryan Carpenter, Rob Rasmussen

It would seem to be an inopportune time in baseball history to be a Soto unless you're the Juan and only. But did you know that Gregory led all Sotos in batting average (minimum, ahem, two at-bats)? To be serious: this Soto has a decent slider but lacks fastball command to get to that good pitch, and for that reason all the batters he faces end up producing like Juan—a condition likely to sentence him to low-leverage pen work, at best. Fastball command is one of those career-long enigmas that can shatter potential into a million tiny ball fours and will remain his nemesis alongside everyone asking him to do the Shuffle.

YEAR	TEAM	LVL	AGE	WHIP	ERA	DRA	WARP	MPH	FB%	WHF	CSP
2017	WMI	A	22	1.29	2.25	3.73	1.7				
2017	LAK	A+	22	1.36	2.25	5.35	0.0				
2018	LAK	A+	23	1.51	4.45	5.53	-0.3				
2019	ERI	AA	24	1.05	2.03	3.70	0.2				
2019	TOL	AAA	24	1.63	6.94	5.19	0.3				
2019	DET	MLB	24	1.86	5.77	7.65	-1.3	98.1	70.7	9.1	51.5
2020	DET	MLB	25	1.66	6.00	5.53	-0.1	97.8	72.4	9.3	52.8

Gregory Soto, continued

Pitch Shape vs LHH

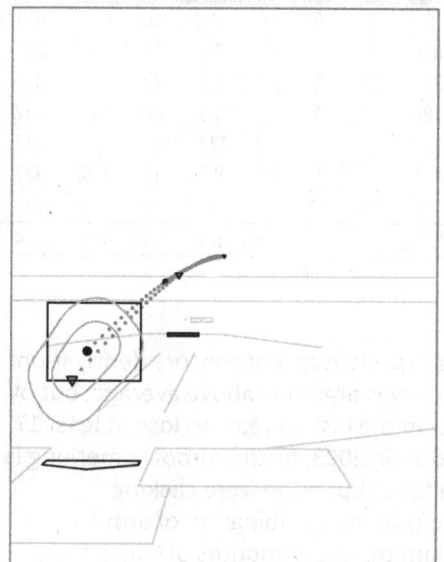

Pitch Shape vs RHH

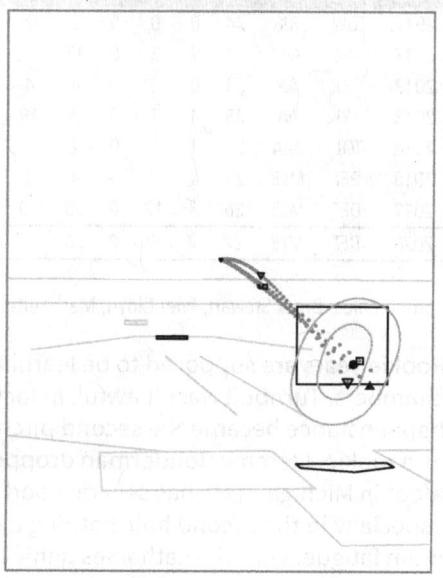

Type	Frequency	Velocity	H Movement	V Movement
● Fastball	65.9%	95.7 [109]	11.2 [81]	-15.6 [101]
☐ Sinker	4.8%	96 [117]	13.1 [97]	-17.3 [111]
+ Cutter				
▲ Changeup	5.5%	88.4 [112]	12.5 [94]	-22.1 [116]
✕ Splitter				
▽ Slider	23.8%	85.2 [103]	-3.1 [92]	-31.2 [105]
◇ Curveball				
⊕ Slow Curveball				
✳ Knuckleball				
▼ Screwball				

Detroit Tigers 2020

Spencer Turnbull   RHP
Born: 09/18/92   Age: 27   Bats: R   Throws: R
Height: 6'3"   Weight: 215   Origin: Round 2, 2014 Draft (#63 overall)

YEAR	TEAM	LVL	AGE	W	L	SV	G	GS	IP	H	HR	BB/9	K/9	K	GB%	BABIP
2017	TGW	RK	24	0	0	0	2	2	9	8	0	2.0	16.0	16	65%	.471
2017	LAK	A+	24	7	3	0	15	15	82^2	68	3	2.7	7.0	64	52%	.280
2017	ERI	AA	24	0	3	0	4	4	20^1	22	1	3.5	9.7	22	58%	.356
2018	ERI	AA	25	4	7	0	19	19	98^2	92	4	3.6	9.6	105	56%	.332
2018	TOL	AAA	25	1	1	0	2	2	13^1	8	0	2.0	12.8	19	57%	.267
2018	DET	MLB	25	0	2	0	4	3	16^1	17	1	2.2	8.3	15	48%	.327
2019	DET	MLB	26	3	17	0	30	30	148^1	154	14	3.6	8.9	146	49%	.333
2020	DET	MLB	27	7	9	0	26	26	130	131	16	3.8	8.9	127	48%	.314

Comparables: Brock Stewart, Tyler Cloyd, Mark Leiter Jr.

Rookie years are supposed to be learning experiences, not sensory deprivation chambers. Turnbull wasn't awful, in fact he was arguably above average, but by happenstance became the second pitcher in the last 40 years to lose at least 17 as a rookie. (Jeremy Bonderman dropped 19 in 2003, further proof something is afoot in Michigan.) He has several good pitches but none were clicking especially in the second half, battling a befuddling combination of arm and brain fatigue. With the catharses behind him thanks to months of wintertime rest, the crimson-chinned chucker ought to be back as a reliable mid-rotation starter.

YEAR	TEAM	LVL	AGE	WHIP	ERA	DRA	WARP	MPH	FB%	WHF	CSP
2017	TGW	RK	24	1.11	4.00	2.21	0.4				
2017	LAK	A+	24	1.12	3.05	4.41	0.8				
2017	ERI	AA	24	1.48	6.20	4.47	0.2				
2018	ERI	AA	25	1.34	4.47	4.22	1.3				
2018	TOL	AAA	25	0.82	2.03	2.90	0.4				
2018	DET	MLB	25	1.29	6.06	4.99	0.1	96.5	63.5	9.9	49.3
2019	DET	MLB	26	1.44	4.61	5.21	0.9	96.2	64.8	11.6	45.3
2020	DET	MLB	27	1.43	4.72	4.55	1.5	95.7	65.5	11.6	47.7

Spencer Turnbull, continued

Pitch Shape vs LHH

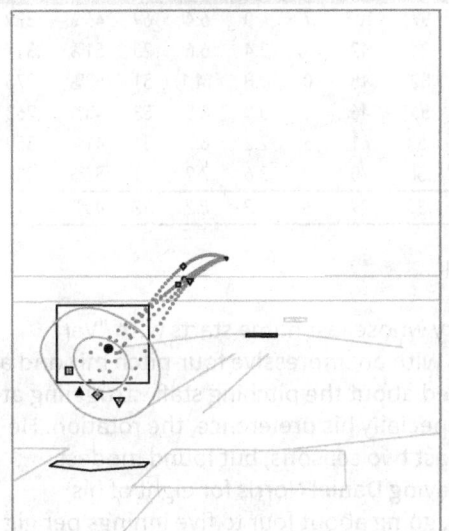

Pitch Shape vs RHH

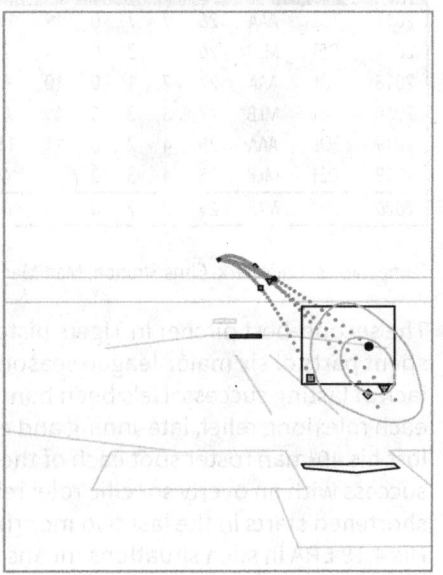

Type	Frequency	Velocity	H Movement	V Movement
● Fastball	44.6%	94 [104]	-1.7 [123]	-17.9 [95]
☐ Sinker	19.4%	94.5 [110]	-13.1 [97]	-21.4 [96]
+ Cutter				
▲ Changeup				
✕ Splitter				
▽ Slider	20.2%	86.7 [110]	4.9 [100]	-32 [103]
◇ Curveball	12.1%	80.6 [107]	10.1 [111]	-49.1 [97]
⊕ Slow Curveball				
✱ Knuckleball				
▼ Screwball				

Drew VerHagen RHP

Born: 10/22/90   Age: 29   Bats: R   Throws: R
Height: 6'6"   Weight: 230   Origin: Round 4, 2012 Draft (#154 overall)

YEAR	TEAM	LVL	AGE	W	L	SV	G	GS	IP	H	HR	BB/9	K/9	K	GB%	BABIP
2017	TOL	AAA	26	7	7	0	19	19	97^1	108	7	4.0	6.4	69	46%	.329
2017	DET	MLB	26	0	3	0	24	2	34^1	42	10	2.4	6.6	25	51%	.317
2018	TOL	AAA	27	2	1	0	10	6	32^2	18	0	2.8	14.1	51	52%	.273
2018	DET	MLB	27	3	3	0	41	1	56^1	46	6	3.0	8.5	53	48%	.263
2019	TOL	AAA	28	4	2	0	11	11	53	61	5	2.2	8.7	51	41%	.350
2019	DET	MLB	28	4	3	0	22	4	58	70	9	3.6	7.9	51	52%	.357
2020	DET	MLB	29	2	2	0	33	0	35	39	6	3.3	8.2	32	48%	.319

Comparables: Chris Beck, Chris Stratton, Matt Magill

The second-best pitcher in Tigers history whose last name starts with "Ver" spent parts of six major-league seasons with an impressive four-pitch mix and a lack of lasting success. He's been bandied about the pitching staff, struggling at each role: long relief, late-inning and especially his preference, the rotation. He lost his 40-man roster spot each of the last two seasons, but found modest success with an overly specific role: relieving Daniel Norris for eight of his shortened starts in the last two months, going about four to five innings per gig. His 4.18 ERA in such situations means either: (a) he's possibly suited for a primary reliever role, or (b) he can get a ride in Norris's van any time he wants.

YEAR	TEAM	LVL	AGE	WHIP	ERA	DRA	WARP	MPH	FB%	WHF	CSP
2017	TOL	AAA	26	1.55	4.90	5.74	0.0				
2017	DET	MLB	26	1.49	5.77	4.95	0.1	95.8	60.5	9.6	50.2
2018	TOL	AAA	27	0.86	1.65	2.11	1.2				
2018	DET	MLB	27	1.15	4.63	3.79	0.8	96.4	54	12.7	46.8
2019	TOL	AAA	28	1.40	4.42	4.62	1.1				
2019	DET	MLB	28	1.60	5.90	5.80	-0.2	95.3	52.9	10.2	49.8
2020	DET	MLB	29	1.47	5.31	5.09	0.0	95.1	54.5	11	48.9

Drew VerHagen, continued

Pitch Shape vs LHH

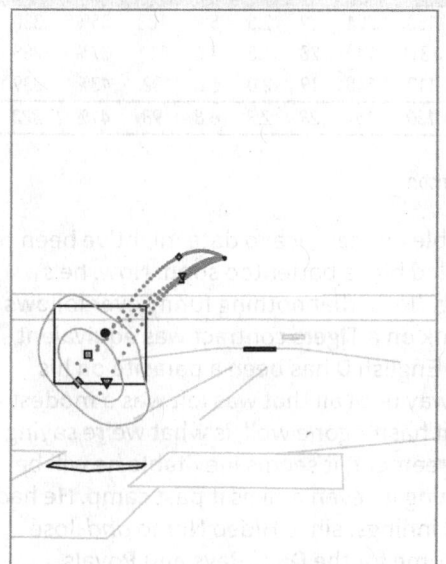

Pitch Shape vs RHH

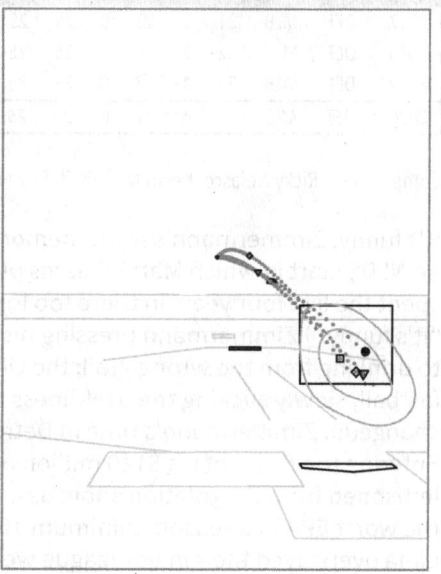

Type	Frequency	Velocity	H Movement	V Movement
● Fastball	12.6%	94.1 [105]	-3.8 [114]	-14.6 [104]
□ Sinker	40.3%	93.2 [103]	-10.9 [111]	-20 [101]
+ Cutter				
▲ Changeup				
✕ Splitter				
▽ Slider	30.5%	85 [102]	8.1 [113]	-33.9 [98]
◇ Curveball	16.3%	78.5 [100]	10.3 [112]	-54.2 [86]
✥ Slow Curveball				
✱ Knuckleball				
▼ Screwball				

Jordan Zimmermann RHP

Born: 05/23/86 Age: 34 Bats: R Throws: R
Height: 6'2" Weight: 225 Origin: Round 2, 2007 Draft (#67 overall)

YEAR	TEAM	LVL	AGE	W	L	SV	G	GS	IP	H	HR	BB/9	K/9	K	GB%	BABIP
2017	DET	MLB	31	8	13	0	29	29	160	204	29	2.5	5.8	103	35%	.330
2018	DET	MLB	32	7	8	0	25	25	131[1]	140	28	1.8	7.6	111	37%	.288
2019	DET	MLB	33	1	13	0	23	23	112	145	19	2.0	6.6	82	43%	.339
2020	DET	MLB	34	6	11	0	26	26	130	161	28	2.3	6.8	98	41%	.322

Comparables: Ricky Nolasco, Kevin Millwood, Erik Hanson

It's funny, Zimmermann's most memorable appearance to date might've been an NLDS start in which Matt Williams pulled him a batter too soon. Now, he's spent the last four years in there too long. (Note that nothing funny ever follows "it's funny.") Zimmermann pressing his ink on a Tigers contract was equivalent to drinking from the wrong grail; the Old English D has been a parasite on his fastball, slowly sucking the usefulness away until all that was left was a modest changeup. Zimmermann's time in Detroit hasn't gone well, is what we're saying. Entering the finale of his $110 million agreement, it seems inevitable he will be jettisoned from the rotation soon, assuming he even makes it past camp. He had the worst ERA in a season, minimum 100 innings, since Hideo Nomo *and* José Lima overstayed their major league welcome for the Devil Rays and Royals, respectively, in 2005. This is a rough denouement to his otherwise honorable career.

YEAR	TEAM	LVL	AGE	WHIP	ERA	DRA	WARP	MPH	FB%	WHF	CSP
2017	DET	MLB	31	1.55	6.07	6.90	-2.4	93.9	54.2	8.8	51.3
2018	DET	MLB	32	1.26	4.52	4.76	0.8	93.0	45.3	9.9	48.2
2019	DET	MLB	33	1.52	6.91	6.74	-1.2	91.9	47	9.5	46.5
2020	DET	MLB	34	1.49	6.15	5.76	-0.2	91.8	47.9	9.3	47.6

Jordan Zimmermann, continued

Pitch Shape vs LHH

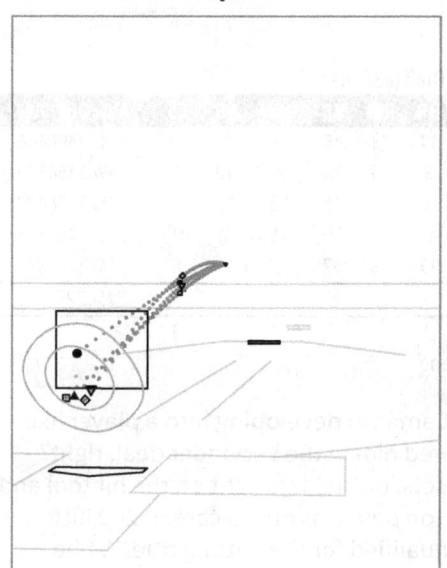

Pitch Shape vs RHH

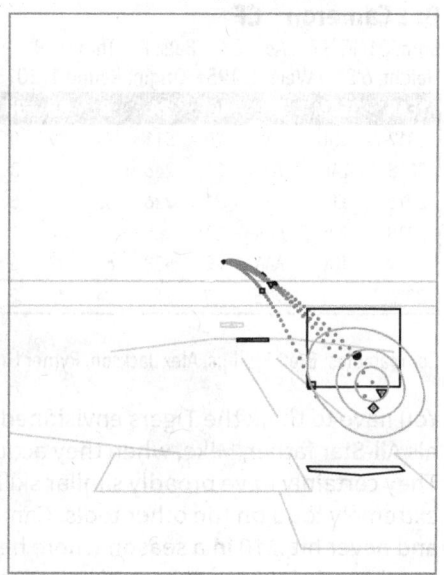

Type	Frequency	Velocity	H Movement	V Movement
● Fastball	34.1%	90.8 [95]	-5.8 [105]	-16.1 [100]
☐ Sinker	12.8%	90.4 [88]	-11 [111]	-23 [91]
+ Cutter				
▲ Changeup				
✕ Splitter				
▽ Slider	31.5%	86.1 [107]	3.3 [93]	-26.5 [119]
◇ Curveball	19.6%	80.5 [106]	5 [90]	-42.2 [111]
⊕ Slow Curveball				
✱ Knuckleball				
▼ Screwball				

Detroit Tigers 2020

PLAYER COMMENTS WITHOUT GRAPHS

Daz Cameron   CF
Born: 01/15/97   Age: 23   Bats: R   Throws: R
Height: 6'2"   Weight: 195   Origin: Round 1, 2015 Draft (#37 overall)

YEAR	TEAM	LVL	AGE	PA	R	2B	3B	HR	RBI	BB	K	SB	CS	AVG/OBP/SLG
2017	QUD	A	20	511	79	29	8	14	73	45	108	32	12	.271/.349/.466
2018	LAK	A+	21	246	35	9	3	3	20	25	69	10	4	.259/.346/.370
2018	ERI	AA	21	226	32	12	5	5	35	25	53	12	5	.285/.367/.470
2018	TOL	AAA	21	62	8	4	1	0	6	2	15	2	2	.211/.246/.316
2019	TOL	AAA	22	528	68	22	6	13	43	62	152	17	8	.214/.330/.377
2020	DET	MLB	23	251	24	12	2	5	25	22	84	9	4	.215/.297/.356

Comparables: Brett Phillips, Alex Jackson, Rymer Liriano

You have to think the Tigers envisioned Cameron developing into a player like his All-Star father, Mike, when they acquired him in the Verlander deal, right? They certainly have broadly similar skill sets: outfielders light on the hit tool and extremely loud on the other tools. Cameron *père* was only a career .249 hitter, and never hit .270 in a season where he qualified for the batting title. Yet he consistently hit for just enough average to let his potent power/speed/glove combination carry the day. After a season-plus of brutal struggles against Triple-A arms, Cameron *fils* needs to substantially improve his bat-to-ball skills to even make it to "just enough." His pops didn't establish himself as a major-league regular until he was 24, so there's a little time left to get back on track, but the sand is starting to pile up at the bottom of the hourglass.

YEAR	TEAM	LVL	AGE	PA	DRC+	VORP	BABIP	BRR	FRAA	WARP
2017	QUD	A	20	511	132	38.5	.323	3.1	CF(110): 1.8, LF(4): -0.7	3.9
2018	LAK	A+	21	246	119	9.9	.366	2.5	CF(38): 1.9, RF(18): 0.9	1.7
2018	ERI	AA	21	226	126	11.4	.366	3.4	CF(34): -7.0, RF(16): 1.5	1.1
2018	TOL	AAA	21	62	52	-1.1	.279	0.7	CF(14): 0.3, RF(1): 0.0	0.0
2019	TOL	AAA	22	528	86	13.1	.291	2.4	CF(92): -1.0, RF(19): 5.4	1.3
2020	DET	MLB	23	251	72	-0.7	.318	0.4	CF 0, RF 1	0.0

Roberto Campos   OF
Born: 06/14/03   Age: 17   Bats: R   Throws: R
Height: 6'3"   Weight: 200   Origin: International Free Agent, 2019

When the Tigers signed Campos last summer for $2.85 million, it was one of the few genuine surprises in the July 2nd international free agent market. Seven-figure July 2nd signees are often publicly "connected" to teams (read: in agreement on early and illegal deals) months to years in advance of becoming official, and deals involving players at this bonus level are almost always known ahead of time. Yet, when the Tigers announced the Campos signing, few knew who he was at all, as he didn't make any of the top July 2 prospect lists. We know he defected from Cuba to the Dominican Republic during a youth baseball tournament in 2016 and trained thereafter with former Tiger-turned-buscone Alex Sánchez, but that's about it. Check back in two or three years to see if he's a real prospect, because we don't have the slightest clue right now.

Riley Greene CF

Born: 09/28/00   Age: 19   Bats: L   Throws: L
Height: 6'3"   Weight: 200   Origin: Round 1, 2019 Draft (#5 overall)

YEAR	TEAM	LVL	AGE	PA	R	2B	3B	HR	RBI	BB	K	SB	CS	AVG/OBP/SLG
2019	TGW	RK	18	43	9	3	0	2	8	5	12	0	0	.351/.442/.595
2019	ONE	A-	18	100	12	3	1	1	7	11	25	1	0	.295/.380/.386
2019	WMI	A	18	108	13	2	2	2	13	6	26	4	0	.219/.278/.344
2020	DET	MLB	19	251	21	11	1	4	22	19	79	3	1	.221/.287/.326

Comparables: Addison Russell, Harold Ramirez, Anthony Gose

Nothing is more enticing than limitless potential. The Tigers were locked in on Greene with the No. 5 pick early in the process, ensorceled by his sweet lefty swing and a high offensive ceiling. He struggled some after an August promotion to Low-A, but also good Lord the kid made full-season ball at 18 in his draft summer. He might grow out of center field as he fills out, and the power is currently more projection than reality—he also might be one of baseball's best prospects in a year or two's time.

YEAR	TEAM	LVL	AGE	PA	DRC+	VORP	BABIP	BRR	FRAA	WARP
2019	TGW	RK	18	43	165	4.9	.478	-1.6	CF(9): -1.9	0.1
2019	ONE	A-	18	100	128	5.7	.403	-1.5	CF(21): 3.5	0.7
2019	WMI	A	18	108	62	1.9	.268	0.8	CF(20): 1.9, RF(4): 0.0	0.2
2020	DET	MLB	19	251	66	-3.1	.322	0.0	CF 3, RF 0	0.0

Chace Numata C

Born: 08/14/92 Age: 27 Bats: B Throws: R
Height: 6'0" Weight: 200 Origin: Round 14, 2010 Draft (#441 overall)

YEAR	TEAM	LVL	AGE	PA	R	2B	3B	HR	RBI	BB	K	SB	CS	AVG/OBP/SLG
2017	REA	AA	24	340	32	17	1	4	28	30	37	0	1	.249/.318/.351
2018	TAM	A+	25	32	7	2	1	1	4	3	4	0	0	.286/.375/.536
2018	TRN	AA	25	135	6	6	1	0	8	7	25	1	1	.180/.222/.242
2019	ERI	AA	26	258	30	11	2	4	26	16	48	0	0	.239/.291/.355
2020									No projection					

"A life is not important except in the impact it has on other lives." — Jackie Robinson

YEAR	TEAM	P. COUNT	FRM RUNS	BLK RUNS	THRW RUNS	TOT RUNS
2017	REA	11602	-3.3	-3.6	0.3	-6.6
2018	TRN	5509	2.1	0.4	-0.7	1.8
2019	ERI	8840	1.0	0.0	1.5	2.4

Chace Numata was selected out of a Hawaiian high school by the Phillies in the 14th round of the 2010 Draft. He kicked around their farm system for the better part of this decade before moving along in minor-league free agency to the Yankees and then the Tigers. He finally made the Triple-A level just this past April, in his 10th pro season. He called games in 2019 for Casey Mize, Matt Manning, Alex Faedo and Tarik Skubal—all of whom are headed toward the big leagues, and soon. He never made one of our prospect lists, and he's never been in this book before. But none of that is important anymore.

Numata passed away in September following a skateboarding accident. He was remembered around baseball as a beloved teammate and friend with an infectious and ever-present smile. He touched many lives around the game and beyond. And in death, he touched five more by giving the gift of life as an organ donor. Rest in peace, Numi.

YEAR	TEAM	LVL	AGE	PA	DRC+	VORP	BABIP	BRR	FRAA	WARP
2017	REA	AA	24	340	83	2.8	.270	-0.7	C(83): -7.9	0.1
2018	TAM	A+	25	32	76	4.2	.304	0.7	C(8): -0.1	0.2
2018	TRN	AA	25	135	35	-6.6	.223	0.2	C(38): 1.3	-0.1
2019	ERI	AA	26	258	82	4.1	.278	-2.7	C(69): 1.2, P(1): 0.0	0.6
2020							No projection			

Detroit Tigers 2020

Isaac Paredes 3B

Born: 02/18/99   Age: 21   Bats: R   Throws: R
Height: 5'11"   Weight: 225   Origin: International Free Agent, 2015

YEAR	TEAM	LVL	AGE	PA	R	2B	3B	HR	RBI	BB	K	SB	CS	AVG/OBP/SLG
2017	SBN	A	18	384	49	25	0	7	49	29	54	2	1	.264/.343/.401
2017	WMI	A	18	133	16	3	0	4	21	13	13	0	0	.217/.323/.348
2018	LAK	A+	19	347	50	19	2	12	48	32	54	1	0	.259/.338/.455
2018	ERI	AA	19	155	20	9	0	3	22	19	22	1	0	.321/.406/.458
2019	ERI	AA	20	552	63	23	1	13	66	57	61	5	3	.282/.368/.416
2020	DET	MLB	21	35	4	2	0	1	4	3	6	0	0	.250/.332/.395

Comparables: Jake Bauers, Ozzie Albies, Cheslor Cuthbert

Welcome to Defensive Spectrum Press Your Luck, baseball's most competitive game. Let's meet today's player, Isaac. He's a 21-year-old with plus bat speed and a knack for hitting who has put up excellent numbers relative to age/league context. He's short and his frame is maxed out, so his range in the infield isn't so hot, and he's already been bouncing around the Big Board trying to find the right home. If Isaac's spin for a long-term position lands on third base or better, he wins an all-expenses paid trip to the majors as a potential first-division regular. If not...well, let's think positive thoughts! Big bucks, no whammies!

YEAR	TEAM	LVL	AGE	PA	DRC+	VORP	BABIP	BRR	FRAA	WARP
2017	SBN	A	18	384	111	18.2	.294	-1.0	SS(70): -2.7, 3B(7): 2.5	1.9
2017	WMI	A	18	133	111	0.3	.214	-0.5	SS(22): -2.4, 3B(5): 1.4	1.1
2018	LAK	A+	19	347	130	24.2	.274	0.3	SS(59): 3.2, 2B(22): 0.5	2.8
2018	ERI	AA	19	155	145	13.7	.358	0.3	3B(18): 0.6, SS(15): 0.9	1.5
2019	ERI	AA	20	552	138	33.2	.298	-2.3	3B(81): -3.4, SS(31): 0.1	3.4
2020	DET	MLB	21	35	91	0.9	.282	-0.1	SS 0	0.1

Beau Burrows RHP

Born: 09/18/96   Age: 23   Bats: R   Throws: R
Height: 6'2"   Weight: 215   Origin: Round 1, 2015 Draft (#22 overall)

YEAR	TEAM	LVL	AGE	W	L	SV	G	GS	IP	H	HR	BB/9	K/9	K	GB%	BABIP
2017	LAK	A+	20	4	3	0	11	11	58^2	45	3	1.7	9.5	62	45%	.298
2017	ERI	AA	20	6	4	0	15	15	76^1	79	5	3.9	8.8	75	40%	.339
2018	ERI	AA	21	10	9	0	26	26	134	126	12	3.8	8.5	127	32%	.310
2019	TOL	AAA	22	2	6	0	15	15	65^1	68	12	4.4	8.4	61	34%	.303
2020	DET	MLB	23	1	1	0	3	3	15	15	2	3.8	7.6	12	35%	.296

Comparables: Luis Ortiz, Lucas Giolito, Zach Lee

You're going to read a lot about shoulder problems in this section of this chapter. This comment will be no different; Burrows missed almost two months in 2019 with shoulder and biceps inflammation. His fastball wasn't all the way back when he returned, continuing a troubling trend of velocity bleed that started in 2018. Any chance of a September call-up to jump start the engines ended with an August oblique strain. His development has stalled out since he made our top 101 list two years ago. It's not what you want, but it's not irreversible.

YEAR	TEAM	LVL	AGE	WHIP	ERA	DRA	WARP	MPH	FB%	WHF	CSP
2017	LAK	A+	20	0.95	1.23	3.38	1.3				
2017	ERI	AA	20	1.47	4.72	5.12	0.0				
2018	ERI	AA	21	1.36	4.10	4.58	1.2				
2019	TOL	AAA	22	1.53	5.51	5.70	0.6				
2020	DET	MLB	23	1.45	4.94	4.84	0.1				

Detroit Tigers 2020

Alex Faedo RHP
Born: 11/12/95   Age: 24   Bats: R   Throws: R
Height: 6'5"   Weight: 230   Origin: Round 1, 2017 Draft (#18 overall)

YEAR	TEAM	LVL	AGE	W	L	SV	G	GS	IP	H	HR	BB/9	K/9	K	GB%	BABIP
2018	LAK	A+	22	2	4	0	12	12	61	49	3	1.9	7.5	51	33%	.263
2018	ERI	AA	22	3	6	0	12	12	60	54	15	3.3	8.9	59	28%	.250
2019	ERI	AA	23	6	7	0	22	22	115^1	104	17	2.0	10.5	134	33%	.293
2020	DET	MLB	24	2	2	0	33	0	35	37	7	3.3	9.1	35	33%	.311

Comparables: Matt Harvey, Jakob Junis, Robert Dugger

Faedo has gotten lost in the shuffle for various reasons. An early candidate to go in the first few picks of the 2017 draft, he slid all the way to No. 18—making him the first-round pitcher chosen by the Tigers a year after Matt Manning and a year before Casey Mize. Faedo isn't in that class of prospect: he doesn't quite throw as hard as he did at the University of Florida; he's been just fine as a pro, neither spectacular enough to gain hype nor bad enough to lose it; and he was the forgotten man in an Erie rotation that was loaded. Yet Faedo is still a cromulent pitching prospect in his own right, with plenty of indicators for future success. He might be flying under the radar now, but the coordinates are still aimed squarely at a rotation spot, and he's closing in fast.

YEAR	TEAM	LVL	AGE	WHIP	ERA	DRA	WARP	MPH	FB%	WHF	CSP
2018	LAK	A+	22	1.02	3.10	3.20	1.5				
2018	ERI	AA	22	1.27	4.95	5.14	0.1				
2019	ERI	AA	23	1.12	3.90	3.75	1.7				
2020	DET	MLB	24	1.41	5.06	5.14	0.0				

Michael Fulmer   RHP

Born: 03/15/93   Age: 27   Bats: R   Throws: R
Height: 6'3"   Weight: 246   Origin: Round 1, 2011 Draft (#44 overall)

YEAR	TEAM	LVL	AGE	W	L	SV	G	GS	IP	H	HR	BB/9	K/9	K	GB%	BABIP
2017	DET	MLB	24	10	12	0	25	25	164^2	150	13	2.2	6.2	114	51%	.273
2018	LAK	A+	25	0	0	0	2	2	6	1	0	0.0	16.5	11	38%	.125
2018	DET	MLB	25	3	12	0	24	24	132^1	128	19	3.1	7.5	110	47%	.288
2020	DET	MLB	27	5	7	0	19	19	99	102	17	3.2	8.1	90	46%	.298

Comparables: Joe Ross, Jered Weaver, Aaron Sanchez

Fulmer should have been prone to an incessant cascade of trade rumors, constantly looking over his shoulder to check the runner as well as the latest tweets suggesting he's drawing interest. Tommy John surgery is a weird way to get out of all that (and unload the uncertainty on to Matthew Boyd in the process) but Fulmer has been a lightning rod of transaction wishcasting ever since being named Rookie of the Year (and subsequently an All-Star), so the long respite might've helped in a weird/bad way. He should be ready for some sweet mound action by the upcoming trade deadline, so he'll miss another season of scuttlebutt and focus on the confidence to throw that slider again.

YEAR	TEAM	LVL	AGE	WHIP	ERA	DRA	WARP	MPH	FB%	WHF	CSP
2017	DET	MLB	24	1.15	3.83	3.75	3.4	98.1	59.4	10.5	48.6
2018	LAK	A+	25	0.17	0.00	1.71	0.3				
2018	DET	MLB	25	1.31	4.69	4.66	1.0	98.3	61	11.7	48.6
2020	DET	MLB	27	1.38	4.81	4.73	0.9	97.7	61	11.3	49.2

Detroit Tigers 2020

Matt Manning   RHP
Born: 01/28/98   Age: 22   Bats: R   Throws: R
Height: 6'6"   Weight: 215   Origin: Round 1, 2016 Draft (#9 overall)

YEAR	TEAM	LVL	AGE	W	L	SV	G	GS	IP	H	HR	BB/9	K/9	K	GB%	BABIP
2017	ONE	A-	19	2	2	0	9	9	33^1	27	0	3.8	9.7	36	31%	.310
2017	WMI	A	19	2	0	0	5	5	17^2	14	0	5.6	13.2	26	49%	.341
2018	WMI	A	20	3	3	0	11	11	55^2	47	3	4.5	12.3	76	43%	.344
2018	LAK	A+	20	4	4	0	9	9	51^1	32	4	3.3	11.4	65	47%	.241
2018	ERI	AA	20	0	1	0	2	2	10^2	11	0	3.4	11.0	13	46%	.393
2019	ERI	AA	21	11	5	0	24	24	133^2	93	7	2.6	10.0	148	48%	.259
2020	DET	MLB	22	2	2	0	33	0	35	34	5	3.6	9.4	37	44%	.307

Comparables: José Berríos, Jake Thompson, Dustin May

When you draft a tall, projectable prep pitcher in the top 10, this is about where you're hoping he is four years down the line. At that point, Manning was an athletic kid with a fastball and curveball that flashed big. It took him awhile to truly get going as a pro—to learn the finer points of command and control, to hone repeatability in his delivery, to sharpen his changeup, all of those small things that separate first-round picks from frontline starters. Things came together quite well in 2019, as Manning was one of the best pitchers in Double-A all season long. He's still a bit of changeup development and more consistency away from being one of the *very* best pitching prospects in the game, but he's in the next tier down. That No. 2 starter outcome is looking quite attainable.

YEAR	TEAM	LVL	AGE	WHIP	ERA	DRA	WARP	MPH	FB%	WHF	CSP
2017	ONE	A-	19	1.23	1.89	4.32	0.4				
2017	WMI	A	19	1.42	5.60	3.60	0.3				
2018	WMI	A	20	1.35	3.40	3.77	0.9				
2018	LAK	A+	20	0.99	2.98	2.71	1.6				
2018	ERI	AA	20	1.41	4.22	4.39	0.1				
2019	ERI	AA	21	0.98	2.56	2.75	3.6				
2020	DET	MLB	22	1.36	4.27	4.41	0.3				

Casey Mize RHP

Born: 05/01/97 Age: 23 Bats: R Throws: R
Height: 6'3" Weight: 220 Origin: Round 1, 2018 Draft (#1 overall)

YEAR	TEAM	LVL	AGE	W	L	SV	G	GS	IP	H	HR	BB/9	K/9	K	GB%	BABIP
2018	LAK	A+	21	0	1	0	4	4	11^2	13	2	1.5	7.7	10	44%	.344
2019	LAK	A+	22	2	0	0	6	6	30^2	11	0	1.5	8.8	30	48%	.155
2019	ERI	AA	22	6	3	0	15	15	78^2	69	5	2.1	8.7	76	42%	.294
2020	DET	MLB	23	2	2	0	33	0	35	35	5	3.0	7.9	31	40%	.292

Comparables: Jackson Stephens, Brett Kennedy, Robert Dugger

Behold, the agony and the ecstasy of the heralded pitching prospect. The No. 1 overall pick in the 2018 draft showed up last spring as a fully-formed good MLB pitcher. He proceeded to decimate batters at the High-A and Double-A levels to the tune of a 0.78 ERA and 2.43 DRA over 78 innings in the first half. By June, he'd emerged into one of the best prospects in the entire sport…just in time to be pulled from a start with a pitcher's most dreaded foe: shoulder inflammation. The injury ultimately cost him only a month of time, but our bigger concern is that he wasn't the same pitcher when he came back. He showed reduced stuff and command, and ran up a 6.61 ERA and 5.86 DRA in 31 innings before being shut down in mid-August. The ultimate fate of Detroit's rebuild may turn on whether the future ace version of Mize resurfaces this year.

YEAR	TEAM	LVL	AGE	WHIP	ERA	DRA	WARP	MPH	FB%	WHF	CSP
2018	LAK	A+	21	1.29	4.63	5.08	0.0				
2019	LAK	A+	22	0.52	0.88	1.83	1.2				
2019	ERI	AA	22	1.11	3.20	4.17	0.8				
2020	DET	MLB	23	1.32	4.33	4.53	0.3				

Detroit Tigers 2020

Matt Moore LHP
Born: 06/18/89   Age: 31   Bats: L   Throws: L
Height: 6'3"   Weight: 210   Origin: Round 8, 2007 Draft (#245 overall)

YEAR	TEAM	LVL	AGE	W	L	SV	G	GS	IP	H	HR	BB/9	K/9	K	GB%	BABIP
2017	SFN	MLB	28	6	15	0	32	31	174[1]	200	27	3.5	7.6	148	39%	.320
2018	TEX	MLB	29	3	8	0	39	12	102	128	19	3.6	7.6	86	39%	.341
2019	DET	MLB	30	0	0	0	2	2	10	3	0	0.9	8.1	9	61%	.130
2020	DET	MLB	31	2	2	0	33	0	35	33	5	3.2	8.0	31	41%	.286

Comparables: Danny Duffy, Jhoulys Chacín, Barry Zito

Much can be said about the "team-friendly extension" and why players should/shouldn't take it, but one unintended consequence is at the completion of the contract, the pitcher is not overpaid and thus very fashionable to sign again. Moore was an All-Star pitcher at the beginning and ended it a hanger-on. After a disappointing turn of events with the Giants, he was dumped on the Rangers with slot money like a single grandmother. Then, on his first year post-Friedman contract, he had two decent starts in Detroit before becoming more like Matt Less thanks to season-ending knee surgery. The lefty was all set for a Something To Prove contract, Take Two even though it's No, Really, I Can Do It This Time, Year Four. Instead, he got a Can't Believe This Guy Is Open To Playing In Asia contract with the Softbank Hawks as he looks to rebuild his value abroad.

YEAR	TEAM	LVL	AGE	WHIP	ERA	DRA	WARP	MPH	FB%	WHF	CSP
2017	SFN	MLB	28	1.53	5.52	5.34	0.4	94.1	51.7	9.4	49.7
2018	TEX	MLB	29	1.66	6.79	7.00	-2.2	94.7	58.7	10.7	52.5
2019	DET	MLB	30	0.40	0.00	4.48	0.1	95.0	53.9	16.2	52.6
2020	DET	MLB	31	1.31	4.12	4.26	0.4	93.5	54.5	10.2	51.5

Franklin Perez RHP

Born: 12/06/97 Age: 22 Bats: R Throws: R
Height: 6'3" Weight: 197 Origin: International Free Agent, 2014

YEAR	TEAM	LVL	AGE	W	L	SV	G	GS	IP	H	HR	BB/9	K/9	K	GB%	BABIP
2017	BCA	A+	19	4	2	2	12	10	54^1	38	4	2.7	8.8	53	38%	.236
2017	CCH	AA	19	2	1	1	7	6	32	33	2	3.1	7.0	25	35%	.316
2018	TGR	RK	20	0	1	0	3	3	8	3	0	0.0	5.6	5	27%	.136
2018	LAK	A+	20	0	1	0	4	4	11^1	15	2	6.4	7.1	9	43%	.371
2019	LAK	A+	21	0	0	0	2	2	7^2	7	1	5.9	7.0	6	46%	.286
2020	DET	MLB	22	2	2	0	33	0	35	35	5	3.6	7.0	27	38%	.287

Comparables: Francis Martes, Brady Lail, Mike Soroka

Perez moved from Houston to Detroit in the Verlander deal, which happened right at the end of the 2017 minor-league season. He was a great get for a waiver trade, or so it seemed at the time, and we ranked him as the No. 53 prospect in baseball that offseason. Since then, he's pitched in a grand total of nine games over two seasons while battling chronic shoulder problems. Meanwhile, as you may already know, Verlander has been the best pitcher in the American League. It seems just a bit less good now, in the same way that *Rocky V* was just a bit less good than the rest of the series.

YEAR	TEAM	LVL	AGE	WHIP	ERA	DRA	WARP	MPH	FB%	WHF	CSP
2017	BCA	A+	19	0.99	2.98	2.76	1.6				
2017	CCH	AA	19	1.38	3.09	4.89	0.1				
2018	TGR	RK	20	0.38	4.50	1.08	0.4				
2018	LAK	A+	20	2.03	7.94	7.67	-0.3				
2019	LAK	A+	21	1.57	2.35	6.15	-0.1				
2020	DET	MLB	22	1.40	4.59	4.62	0.2				

Detroit Tigers 2020

Tarik Skubal   LHP

Born: 11/20/96   Age: 23   Bats: L   Throws: L
Height: 6'3"   Weight: 215   Origin: Round 9, 2018 Draft (#255 overall)

YEAR	TEAM	LVL	AGE	W	L	SV	G	GS	IP	H	HR	BB/9	K/9	K	GB%	BABIP
2018	ONE	A-	21	0	0	1	4	0	12	8	0	1.5	12.8	17	46%	.333
2018	WMI	A	21	2	0	1	3	0	7^1	5	0	1.2	13.5	11	29%	.357
2019	LAK	A+	22	4	5	0	15	15	80^1	62	5	2.1	10.9	97	40%	.292
2019	ERI	AA	22	2	3	0	9	9	42^1	25	2	3.8	17.4	82	41%	.343
2020	DET	MLB	23	2	2	0	33	0	35	34	5	3.4	11.8	46	40%	.341

Comparables: Taylor Rogers, Adam Morgan, Dylan Cease

If you love lefties who throw gorgeous curveballs—and who doesn't?—meet your new favorite artist. Skubal had just a little buzz coming into 2019 as a lefty with good stuff whose college career was marred by Tommy John surgery. After a true breakout campaign, he's emerged as a top prospect, with a full four-pitch mix fronted by a mid-90s heater. The true star of the band is his curve, which has a chance to be one of Detroit's best hooks since the heyday of Motown. Because of the injury history and all the usual questions about pitching prospects, we don't know whether the final cut will be starter or reliever as of yet. We think it'll be a great album either way.

YEAR	TEAM	LVL	AGE	WHIP	ERA	DRA	WARP	MPH	FB%	WHF	CSP
2018	ONE	A-	21	0.83	0.75	3.08	0.2				
2018	WMI	A	21	0.82	0.00	2.52	0.2				
2019	LAK	A+	22	1.01	2.58	3.31	1.7				
2019	ERI	AA	22	1.02	2.13	2.40	1.3				
2020	DET	MLB	23	1.36	4.35	4.45	0.3				

Joey Wentz LHP

Born: 10/06/97 Age: 22 Bats: L Throws: L
Height: 6'5" Weight: 210 Origin: Round 1, 2016 Draft (#40 overall)

YEAR	TEAM	LVL	AGE	W	L	SV	G	GS	IP	H	HR	BB/9	K/9	K	GB%	BABIP
2017	ROM	A	19	8	3	0	26	26	131^2	99	4	3.1	10.4	152	41%	.293
2018	BRV	A+	20	3	4	0	16	16	67	49	3	3.2	7.1	53	46%	.250
2019	MIS	AA	21	5	8	0	20	20	103	90	13	3.9	8.7	100	35%	.280
2019	ERI	AA	21	2	0	0	5	5	25^2	20	3	1.4	13.0	37	19%	.315
2020	DET	MLB	22	2	2	0	33	0	35	35	5	3.7	8.4	33	34%	.300

Comparables: Danny Duffy, Giovanni Soto, Alex Torres

Wentz was one of the best prospects moved at the 2019 trade deadline. It was a slow deadline and everyone hugged top prospects like their favorite childhood stuffed animal, true, yet the Tigers nabbed this promising and touted young southpaw for Shane Greene's extremely shiny and totally unsustainable ERA. Sure enough, Greene went back to being a decent if unspectacular reliever the moment he landed with Atlanta, and Wentz ripped off one of the best months of his career in his new system. This is the type of sneaky deal that can separate successful rebuilds from perpetual mediocrity.

YEAR	TEAM	LVL	AGE	WHIP	ERA	DRA	WARP	MPH	FB%	WHF	CSP
2017	ROM	A	19	1.10	2.60	2.78	3.9				
2018	BRV	A+	20	1.09	2.28	3.46	1.5				
2019	MIS	AA	21	1.31	4.72	5.50	-0.7				
2019	ERI	AA	21	0.94	2.10	3.28	0.5				
2020	DET	MLB	22	1.40	4.54	4.65	0.2				

Detroit Tigers 2020

LINEOUTS

Hitters

HITTER	POS	TEAM	LVL	AGE	PA	R	2B	3B	HR	RBI	BB	K	SB	CS	AVG/OBP/SLG	DRC+	WARP
Sergio Alcántara	SS	ERI	AA	22	378	46	10	0	2	27	48	71	7	6	.247/.346/.296	101	2.2
Jorge Bonifacio	RF	KCA	MLB	26	21	3	3	0	0	3	1	7	0	0	.350/.381/.500	67	-0.1
	RF	OMA	AAA	26	500	67	18	5	20	62	38	121	6	4	.222/.284/.417	74	0.8
Eric Haase	C	CLE	MLB	26	17	1	0	0	1	3	1	8	0	0	.063/.118/.250	72	-0.1
	C	COH	AAA	26	401	67	12	3	28	60	42	142	1	1	.226/.315/.517	93	1.9
Derek Hill	OF	ERI	AA	23	526	78	19	5	14	45	38	147	21	13	.243/.311/.394	92	2.2
Pete Kozma	SS	TOL	AAA	31	322	44	17	2	7	51	32	49	2	0	.263/.340/.414	99	1.9
Parker Meadows	CF	WMI	A	19	504	52	15	2	7	40	47	113	14	8	.221/.296/.312	78	0.0
Wenceel Perez	SS	WMI	A	19	516	59	16	6	3	30	45	87	21	13	.233/.299/.314	78	-0.4
Dustin Peterson	RF	DET	MLB	24	47	3	4	0	0	6	2	14	1	0	.227/.277/.318	62	-0.2
	RF	TOL	AAA	24	319	31	13	0	11	49	14	78	1	1	.286/.317/.439	91	-0.7
Nick Quintana	3B	WMI	A	21	162	14	5	1	1	13	13	51	3	1	.158/.228/.226	37	-0.1
	3B	ONE	A-	21	98	12	7	0	1	4	12	31	1	0	.256/.347/.372	130	0.3
Jacob Robson	OF	TOL	AAA	24	473	61	21	3	9	52	53	132	25	10	.267/.352/.399	97	0.8
Frank Schwindel	1B	ERI	AA	27	188	21	8	0	5	23	11	27	0	0	.257/.309/.392	98	-0.1
	1B	OMA	AAA	27	76	8	4	0	1	10	4	13	0	1	.186/.237/.286	36	-0.5
	1B	TOL	AAA	27	119	21	7	0	9	33	6	19	0	0	.327/.361/.628	150	0.8
	1B	KCA	MLB	27	15	0	0	0	0	0	0	2	0	0	.067/.067/.067	83	0.0
Troy Stokes	LF	SAN	AAA	23	381	50	22	0	9	40	47	87	14	3	.233/.341/.385	90	0.1
Bobby Wilson	C	TOL	AAA	36	101	12	2	0	5	10	11	25	0	0	.244/.327/.433	101	1.3
	C	DET	MLB	36	47	2	1	0	0	2	2	11	0	0	.091/.130/.114	60	0.2

Here's our annual reminder that **Sergio Alcántara** is still on track for a career as a glove-first utility player. ⓧ **Jorge Bonifacio** started 122 games during the 2019 season; granted, 117 of them were at Triple-A, but statistically it still seems fairly damning. ⓧ The good: **Eric Haase** socked 28 dingers in Triple-A, tied for fifth in the International League. The bad: Despite the pop, he hit .226 and really struggled framing behind the dish. The ugly: In a 10-game cup of coffee, the backup backstop fell to strikes almost half the time. Maybe he should go by Haaaase? ⓧ Now five years removed from his one and presumably only appearance on the BP 101, former first-rounder **Derek Hill** keeps hitting *just* enough to maintain a slight bit of prospect relevancy. ⓧ In November 2018, the Perth Heat of the Australian Baseball League announced the signing of "MLB star **Pete Kozma**" for the winter campaign. In the Northern Hemisphere, he continues to be "Quad-A utility man who inexplicably was the starting shortstop for the Cards that one year Pete Kozma." ⓧ **Parker Meadows** shares a sweet lefty swing and a big set of athletic tools with older brother Austin. Whether he also got any of the family hitting ability is still unclear. ⓧ **Wenceel Perez** had a rough offensive campaign as a teenager in Low-A, and yet playing the entire summer as a teenager in full-season ball is a significant accomplishment in and of itself. He still has quite a bit of time for the offensive tools to pull together. ⓧ **Dustin Peterson** opened the season as a semi-regular in Detroit for a hot second, and might eventually stick somewhere as a fourth outfielder. ⓧ Second-rounder **Nick Quintana** struggled so badly at the Low-A level after signing that he was demoted to short-season ball in August. He'll get something of a pass for being at the end of a long college campaign, but it wasn't encouraging for someone advertised as a polished college power bat. ⓧ **Jacob Robson** grew up a Tigers fan in neighboring Windsor, Ontario. He didn't quite get to Detroit this year, but his old-school leadoff profile should play in the majors soon. ⓧ Trivia note for future generations: the Opening Day first baseman for the 2019 Royals was **Frank Schwindel**, making his major-league debut. He was sent down by Tax Day and released in May, ending up on an odyssey that included stops at four levels in two organizations. ⓧ **Troy Stokes** has an intriguing basket of tools that includes both power and speed. His home-run production sharply dipped in 2019, even though he was moving to the new power-mad environment in Triple-A, and he was claimed off waivers in September. If you write his name out in full—Troy Stokes Junior—it doubles as a sentence. ⓧ If you're going to spend the twilight of a long, occasionally successful career hoping for an emergency call-up while hanging around Triple-A as a backup catcher, it's important to pick the right organization. **Bobby Wilson**—or "BMW," per his chest protector—now has a two-year streak of choosing wisely.

Detroit Tigers 2020

Pitchers

PITCHER	TEAM	LVL	AGE	W	L	SV	G	GS	IP	H	HR	BB/9	K/9	K	GB%	WHIP	ERA	DRA	WARP
Austin Adams	ROC	AAA	32	1	1	1	11	1	18	16	3	3.0	14.0	28	60%	1.22	4.50	5.41	0.2
	TOL	AAA	32	0	2	1	18	1	25^2	26	6	3.5	7.0	20	46%	1.40	6.66	5.37	0.2
	MIN	MLB	32	0	0	0	2	0	2^2	4	2	10.1	16.9	5	43%	2.62	16.88	5.32	0.0
	DET	MLB	32	0	0	0	13	0	14	14	2	6.4	5.8	9	41%	1.71	5.14	7.80	-0.4
Victor Alcantara	TOL	AAA	26	0	0	0	13	2	18^1	17	3	2.9	7.9	16	59%	1.25	5.89	4.07	0.4
	DET	MLB	26	3	2	0	46	0	42^2	45	8	3.2	5.1	24	55%	1.41	4.85	5.62	-0.1
Sandy Baez	TOL	AAA	25	1	0	0	18	0	22	27	1	5.7	7.4	18	34%	1.86	7.36	6.72	-0.1
	DET	MLB	25	0	0	0	1	0	1	2	0	0.0	0.0	0	40%	2.00	9.00	5.90	0.0
Ryan Carpenter	TOL	AAA	28	5	7	0	14	14	77	77	11	3.0	8.9	76	42%	1.34	5.26	4.74	1.5
	DET	MLB	28	1	6	0	9	9	40^2	61	12	2.9	5.5	25	38%	1.82	9.30	9.03	-1.4
Anthony Castro	ERI	AA	24	5	3	1	27	18	102^1	75	9	5.7	10.2	116	45%	1.37	4.40	4.78	0.2
Jose Fernandez	ERI	AA	26	1	3	1	11	3	26	30	4	2.4	6.6	19	27%	1.42	4.15	5.84	-0.3
	TOL	AAA	26	1	1	0	27	1	34^2	40	5	4.2	6.2	24	39%	1.62	5.97	6.58	-0.1
	DET	MLB	26	0	0	0	4	0	3^2	6	1	12.3	4.9	2	20%	3.00	17.18	8.35	-0.1
Kyle Funkhouser	ERI	AA	25	3	1	0	4	4	23^2	16	2	1.1	11.0	29	45%	0.80	1.90	2.81	0.6
	TOL	AAA	25	3	7	0	18	18	63^1	79	3	7.7	9.2	65	54%	2.10	8.53	7.79	-0.7
Bryan Garcia	TOL	AAA	24	3	0	0	31	0	33^1	26	4	3.8	8.9	33	46%	1.20	2.97	3.79	0.8
	DET	MLB	24	0	0	0	7	0	6^2	9	1	6.8	9.4	7	62%	2.10	12.15	4.83	0.0
Rony Garcia	TAM	A+	21	0	2	0	5	4	25	21	2	2.5	9.0	25	34%	1.12	2.16	4.03	0.3
	TRN	AA	21	4	11	0	20	20	105^1	94	14	3.2	8.9	104	35%	1.25	4.44	5.52	-0.7
Carlos Guzman	WMI	A	21	2	2	0	7	7	33	23	3	4.9	7.4	27	47%	1.24	2.73	3.89	0.5
Matt Hall	TOL	AAA	25	5	4	0	25	13	86^2	102	16	3.2	11.0	106	50%	1.53	5.30	5.72	0.7
	DET	MLB	25	0	1	0	16	0	23^1	28	4	5.8	10.4	27	39%	1.84	7.71	5.71	-0.1
Wilkel Hernandez	WMI	A	20	9	7	0	21	21	101^1	97	5	2.3	8.0	90	40%	1.21	3.73	4.05	1.4
Eduardo Jimenez	TOL	AAA	24	4	3	2	41	0	54^2	39	5	3.0	8.4	51	47%	1.04	2.96	3.00	1.7
	DET	MLB	24	0	0	0	8	0	10^2	12	1	4.2	6.8	8	39%	1.59	5.91	6.14	-0.1
Alex Lange	MYR	A+	23	1	9	0	11	11	47^2	58	4	4.9	9.6	51	52%	1.76	7.36	7.04	-1.2
	TEN	AA	23	2	3	0	7	7	39	36	4	4.4	6.5	28	47%	1.41	3.92	5.82	-0.5
	ERI	AA	23	2	1	0	9	0	15^2	13	0	4.6	8.6	15	47%	1.34	3.45	5.46	-0.1
David McKay	TAC	AAA	24	3	1	1	30	0	43^2	31	4	6.4	14.6	71	32%	1.42	5.15	2.88	1.4
	SEA	MLB	24	0	0	0	7	0	7	5	1	10.3	6.4	5	33%	1.86	5.14	8.22	-0.2
	DET	MLB	24	0	0	0	18	0	19^1	15	2	4.2	13.5	29	26%	1.24	5.59	3.59	0.4

PITCHER	TEAM	LVL	AGE	W	L	SV	G	GS	IP	H	HR	BB/9	K/9	K	GB%	WHIP	ERA	DRA	WARP
Zac Reininger	TOL	AAA	26	4	3	0	34	4	57^1	65	7	4.1	8.0	51	44%	1.59	4.08	5.55	0.5
	DET	MLB	26	0	3	0	25	1	28	44	11	5.1	5.5	17	38%	2.14	8.68	9.91	-1.4
Paul Richan	MYR	A+	22	10	5	0	17	17	93	96	10	1.7	8.3	86	40%	1.23	3.97	4.90	0.1
	LAK	A+	22	2	2	0	5	5	30^2	39	2	0.6	8.5	29	43%	1.34	4.11	6.73	-0.6
Elvin Rodriguez	LAK	A+	21	11	9	0	24	23	133^2	113	12	3.0	7.5	112	37%	1.17	3.77	4.88	0.2
John Schreiber	ERI	AA	25	0	0	0	5	0	7	4	1	3.9	15.4	12	57%	1.00	2.57	2.92	0.1
	TOL	AAA	25	6	4	4	48	0	59^1	39	4	3.2	10.6	70	42%	1.01	2.28	2.40	2.2
	DET	MLB	25	2	0	0	13	0	13	16	3	2.8	13.2	19	37%	1.54	6.23	5.02	0.0
Daniel Stumpf	TOL	AAA	28	2	1	4	14	0	15^1	8	0	2.3	14.1	24	32%	0.78	0.59	1.39	0.7
	DET	MLB	28	1	1	0	48	0	29	35	5	4.7	8.7	28	37%	1.72	4.34	7.22	-0.6
Alex Wilson	SAN	AAA	32	4	1	2	29	0	38	33	8	1.7	7.3	31	51%	1.05	2.13	3.91	0.9
	IOW	AAA	32	1	2	1	10	0	12^1	12	2	1.5	8.0	11	51%	1.14	5.11	5.50	0.1
	MIL	MLB	32	1	1	1	13	0	11^1	15	3	7.1	10.3	13	40%	2.12	9.53	5.14	0.0

Austin Adams still approaches 100 mph on the radar gun despite being well into his 30s. He also still gets clobbered every time he makes it back to the majors. It's nice when people stay true to their roots. ⓪ Sinkerballer **Victor Alcántara** had injured list stints in 2019 for a wisdom tooth extraction and a finger contusion. There's a third condition that isn't health related that's a bigger threat to his place on the active roster: his stuff doesn't fool MLB hitters. ⓪ **Sandy Baez** provides a slightly different spin on the generic 95-and-a-slider up-and-down reliever by mixing in a foshball, an old-timey name for a split-change. ⓪ Fringe southpaw **Ryan Carpenter**'s career 8.57 ERA is the eighth worst in MLB history, minimum 60 innings. Conversely, Ryan Baseball is one of the worst-rated contractors in the metro area, minimum one-and-a-half Yelp stars. ⓪ Not to be confused with the other Castro in the Tigers system, or the other-other Castro in the Tigers system, **Anthony Castro** is a pitcher. Like the other Castro's, his fringy stuff has the floor to reach the big leagues and that's about it. ⓪ This **José Fernández** shares a name and an approximate velocity band with the late Marlins ace but little else. He's a lefty reliever who needs some things to break right to get a steady LOOGY paycheck. The three-batter minimum rule is an extinction-level threat to his career. ⓪ **Kyle Funkhouser** has battled a long string of injuries encompassing everything from vague shoulder soreness to a broken foot from bad concrete on a sidewalk. The stuff still flashes enough to have a bit of hope, but it's fading fast. ⓪ Former University of Miami closer **Bryan Garcia** had a successful return from 2018 Tommy John surgery, earning a September call-up. As relief prospects go, he's mildly interesting. ⓪ Converted infielder **Carlos Guzman** was just starting to make waves as a pitching prospect when he went down with an elbow injury in May and missed the rest of the season. His athleticism and changeup make him one worth watching. ⓪ Were the late poet Donald Hall to write a lineout concerning soft-tossing lefty **Matt**

Detroit Tigers 2020

Hall, he might go with something like: "It's almost relaxing to know he'll be designated for assignment fairly soon, as it's a comfort not to obsess about his next failed big-league stint." ⚾ One of two live arms acquired in a 2017 trade with the Angels for Ian Kinsler, **Wilkel Hernandez** has a starter's frame and worked all season at High-A to decent results. How the secondaries develop as he progresses through the system will determine if he can stick in a rotation. ⚾ "It's just a dream. I still do not believe that I am finally here," reliever **Eduardo Jiménez** told Chris McCosky of *The Detroit News* after he was called up in May. "Since I was a kid I dreamed about this." We should always remember that making the majors is the culmination of a lifetime of dreams and hard work, even for an up-and-down reliever. ⚾ Former Cubs first-rounder **Alex Lange** moved to the Tigers system in the Nicholas Castellanos trade; he was the more famous of the two prospects moved, but the lesser one by the time of the deal. Detroit converted him to relief after acquiring him, and he pitched much better in that role. ⚾ Curveball specialist and Florida Atlantic alum **David McKay** was an August waiver claim by the Tigers from the Mariners, which is about as depressing as a 2019 baseball transaction can get. Roll Owls. ⚾ **Zac Reininger** has the same initials and letter count as *Final Sacrifice* antihero Zap Rowsdower, and both prove you need more than decent mechanics and questionable '90s stuff. ⚾ **Paul Richan**, the better prospect from the Castellanos deal, is one of the best command-and-control pitching prospects in the minors. Some guys with this profile turn into good major league starters, and some of them turn into human JUGS machines. ⚾ Once upon a time, **Elvin Rodriguez** was an interesting but very skinny pitching prospect traded for Justin Upton. He's older now—aren't we all—but remains an interesting prospect who is as thick as a bow string. He'll face the Double-A test in 2020. ⚾ The stars of *I Love Lucy* and *The Six Million Dollar Man* share a hometown of Wyandotte, Michigan with Downriver Detroit denizen **John Schreiber**. That explains why his deceptive sidearm delivery got him a callup to play Ball in the Majors. ⚾ **Daniel Stumpf** has built a career of not being able to handle righties at all, which explains spending much of his spare time volunteering for the Hillary Clinton campaign. ⚾ **Alex Wilson** has reached the "gotta sign a minor-league deal with the Tigers" portion of his unremarkable but solid career. We don't feel the need to pile on further.

Tigers Prospects

The State of the System

It's a very good top three, a pretty good top five, and then, well the system is not nearly as deep as you'd want at this point in the uh "planned reconstruction process."

The Top Ten

─────── ★ ★ ★ *2020 Top 101 Prospect* **#12** ★ ★ ★ ───────

1 **Casey Mize   RHP**   OFP: 70   ETA: 2020
Born: 05/01/97   Age: 23   Bats: R   Throws: R   Height: 6'3"   Weight: 220
Origin: Round 1, 2018 Draft (#1 overall)

The Report: Healthy 2019 Casey Mize had a strong argument for the best pitching prospect in baseball. He'll show four plus pitches, and each of the fastball, cutter, slider and split will flash plus-plus at times. The fastball can sit around 94, but there's 97 with life when he needs it. He'll manipulate a mid-80s slider from a true 11-5 bat misser, to a slurvier low-80s option to spot. The mid-80s split has good fade and tumble. The cutter is around 90 and has tight, late cut to induce weak contact. There's plus command of everything. Every prospect writer on staff that saw Mize preferred a different secondary, which means it could all come together one day as a monster top-of-the-rotation starter.

Then in June Mize was shut down for a month with what was termed "shoulder inflammation." There were arm concerns going back to his college days, and his arm action has some late effort. I'm not a huge fan of it generally, although he repeats it fine enough. Mize didn't look like the same pitcher after coming back and was shut down a few weeks early. If we had high confidence he would have a healthy, full 2020, he'd rank as the best pitching prospect in baseball. But we don't. If he'd been healthy all of 2019, he might have pitched himself to the majors and out of prospect list consideration. He didn't. Pitchers, man.

Variance: High. Is he healthy? Tune in during spring training to maybe find out!

Mark Barry's Fantasy Take: Yikes. Mize might represent the biggest chasm between ceiling and floor in the minors. That's hyperbole, sure, but with health he could be one of the five best arms in the league. The problem is he's a pitcher and in addition to possessing the skills to get dudes out he also has a knack for picking up nagging arm injuries. He's still one of the best pitching prospects in the game, but the risk is high enough to keep him out of the top spot.

★ ★ ★ *2020 Top 101 Prospect* **#47** ★ ★ ★

2 Matt Manning RHP   OFP: 60   ETA: 2020/21
Born: 01/28/98 Age: 22 Bats: R Throws: R Height: 6'6" Weight: 215
Origin: Round 1, 2016 Draft (#9 overall)

The Report: Three years after drafting Manning as a somewhat baseball-raw, very projectable prep arm, you'd imagine the Tigers have to be fairly pleased with where he is now. It wasn't the most direct route to top-50 prospectdom, mind you. His delivery has vastly changed over the last 24 months from uptempo, uphill, drop and drive mechanics that didn't make good use of his height—and that he couldn't consistently repeat—to a smoother, more upright and repeatable delivery that makes better use of all of his 6-foot-6 length. His fastball generally sits in an average velo band, touching 96 or occasionally higher, but the serious extension and tough angle make it play up. Manning can throw the fastball to both sides of the plate consistently, and move it in or out. The curve can get humpy and he will still slow his arm action on it at times, but it will also flash plus-plus in the upper 70s, and he can manipulate the shape from a true 12-6 downer to a backfoot 12-5 to lefties. The change remains the third pitch, too firm with below-average command. He'll turn over a few nice ones, but it's still in the "needs a grade jump to start" range. We think he'll get close enough with it, and he's a better bet to be a mid-rotation arm now than this time last year.

Variance: Medium. There's still some relief risk. The change might not get there, he's got a lot of limbs to keep in line, and mechanical inconsistency has been a problem in the past. He's shown more fastball occasionally in the past though, and it's not impossible the fastball jumps as he continues to figure things out and the profile plays up past this.

Mark Barry's Fantasy Take: Wait, did I already do to "huge discrepancy between floor and ceiling" bit? Manning's bugaboo is a little less injury-related than Mize's (although there's injury risk because, you know, pitchers) and pertains more to his changeup. He can still be effective with a mediocre change, but as a 2.5-pitch pitcher, his fantasy upside slides to back-end starter or late-inning reliever. His proximity and potential keeps him in the top-50ish, however.

★ ★ ★ *2020 Top 101 Prospect* **#49** ★ ★ ★

3 Riley Greene OF   OFP: 60   ETA: 2023
Born: 09/28/00 Age: 19 Bats: L Throws: L Height: 6'3" Weight: 200
Origin: Round 1, 2019 Draft (#5 overall)

The Report: Greene is a toolsy prep outfielder with a better present hit tool than the average member of that cohort. He loads late but keeps everything in sync well, and has plus bat speed with slight lift to his swing. The contact makes that sound and while he has a crude approach against offspeed at present, it is projectable, and he'll foul off a tough curve here and there, or stay back on a change and flick it into right field. You'll get enough glimpses to project a plus hit tool at maturity. There's above-average pull-side raw—which will end up plus—and he may grow into all-fields power in his twenties. Greene is not going to sell out for pop—when he does the swing gets long with some wrap—so projects more as a 20-homer guy than a 30-homer guy. He's an above-average runner at present, but is likely to slow down as he ages, and his routes and reads in the outfield are very rough. This might force him to left field—due to below-average arm strength—by the majors. That will put added pressure on the bat, but it's a very good bat.

Variance: High. He may end up in a corner, and it's not a huge power projection play, more a well-balanced offensive skill set, and one that hasn't really been tested as a pro yet.

Mark Barry's Fantasy Take: Spreading your age-18 season across three levels is likely quite the whirlwind, so let's take Greene's stat lines with a grain of salt. I like this guy quite a bit, and am looking forward to him sticking to a level for longer than 108 plate appearances. At his peak, he'll flirt with .300 with 20-25 homers and could even sneak in double-digit steals until he grows out of it. For fantasy purposes, I might have Greene slightly higher than Manning.

─── ★ ★ ★ *2020 Top 101 Prospect* **#76** ★ ★ ★ ───

4
Tarik Skubal LHP OFP: 55 ETA: 2020
Born: 11/20/96 Age: 23 Bats: L Throws: L Height: 6'3" Weight: 215
Origin: Round 9, 2018 Draft (#255 overall)

The Report: Skubal was a bit of an afterthought as a ninth-round pick in 2018, but the Tigers were taking a flyer on a lefty still recovering from Tommy John surgery in 2017. That gamble paid off in spades as Skubal showed off a mid-90s fastball with plenty of movement and improved command across two levels last year. His slider also flashed plus, giving him a dynamic two-pitch mix that gives him both excellent potential as a starter and a floor as an impact reliever. There's potential in his changeup that flashes above-average, but he needs consistency in his second full season. Skubal will also mix a curveball in a times, showing a slower upper-70s bender that proves effective working off his harder fastball and slider. Proving his command improvement is here to stay and allowing an additional tick on his changeup could still push Skubal slightly past this OFP.

Variance: Medium. His pro track record is still pretty short and there's work to do with the changeup, but the lightning fast gain in command has improved this portion of the profile dramatically.

Detroit Tigers 2020

Mark Barry's Fantasy Take: It's a bit of a cliché that the command is the last thing to come back after Tommy John surgery, and it's also a bit of a cliché to say that these things are clichés for a reason. Anyway, now that a semblance of Skubal's command has returned, we can dream on him being a high-strikeout SP3-type, which is probably good for the back end of the 101.

5 Joey Wentz   LHP   OFP: 55   ETA: 2020
Born: 10/06/97   Age: 22   Bats: L   Throws: L   Height: 6'5"   Weight: 210
Origin: Round 1, 2016 Draft (#40 overall)

The Report: After an injury-plagued 2018 campaign during which he often didn't have a good fastball, Wentz bounced back last year in Double-A. Now healthy, he sat low 90s again with late arm-side run. He is effective changing eye levels with the pitch, and it has some riding life up due to his height and high-three-quarters slot. A deceptive arm action adds to the effective velocity of the fastball as well. Wentz can struggle at times with the consistency of his breaking ball. It will vacillate between a 12-6 curve and something slurvier. The command of the breaker will come and go as well, but it does flash above-average when he's on top of it. The changeup has become a real weapon against righties and he can fade it off the plate away or cut and sink it inside. There may not be a future plus pitch here anymore, but it's a solid-average arsenal from the southpaw and he looked especially effective mixing his stuff post-trade.

Variance: Medium. Outside of his injury-plagued 2018, Wentz has been fairly durable and held his own as a 21-year-old in Double-A. He may not quite have the same upside we saw two years ago in A-ball, but he's a good bet to be a useful major league rotation piece of the Tigers.

Mark Barry's Fantasy Take: Wentz was awesome in five starts after infiltrating the Tigers organization, but I'm still not sure he has quite the same upside as the three arms above him on this list. Solid fantasy SP4, yes. More? Perhaps not.

6 Isaac Paredes   SS   OFP: 50   ETA: 2021
Born: 02/18/99   Age: 21   Bats: R   Throws: R   Height: 5'11"   Weight: 225
Origin: International Free Agent, 2015

The Report: Paredes was the centerpiece of a 2017 deadline deal that shipped two journeymen players to the Cubs for the stretch run. He's hit at every level thanks to an exceptional ability to recognize spin and detailed knowledge of the strike zone. His ability to track pitches allows him to find hitter's counts and utilize his barrel control to drive the ball. The contact isn't often loud enough to project him as a future plus-plus hitter, but it wouldn't be a stretch to see an above-average hitter with average pop, mostly to the pull side. A below-average runner with below-average range on the dirt, Paredes doesn't project to stay up the middle, putting additional pressure on his solid, if unspectacular, bat. Though he continues to play shortstop, he has seen time at both second and third base, where his ability flashes a touch better, but still inconsistently. Paredes owns a difficult profile where he must walk a fine line to play enough of a defensive position for his bat to hold up and make him a worthwhile regular.

Variance: Medium. His defensive home remains an open question and the bat may not completely support a move too far down the defensive spectrum.

Mark Barry's Fantasy Take: It feels like Paredes has been around forever (or maybe that's just me), but somehow he's still just 20 years old. Lucky for us, we're not too concerned with defense and I get serious Jhonny Peralta, Eduardo Escobar (thanks, Ben) and good-Mark Derosa-y vibes here. While .275 with 20 homers doesn't knock your socks off, it's still pretty useful, especially in deeper and only leagues.

7. Alex Faedo   RHP
OFP: 50   ETA: 2020
Born: 11/12/95   Age: 24   Bats: R   Throws: R   Height: 6'5"   Weight: 230
Origin: Round 1, 2017 Draft (#18 overall)

The Report: Faedo's prospect stock has taken a tumble the last two years largely because he hasn't proven to be the pitcher fans fell in love with during the College World Series. Once you get past those memories and focus on what he is today, Faedo is a perfectly acceptable back-end pitching prospect. His fastball sits consistently in the 89-91 mph range, though he will reach for 93 or 94 on occasion. That said, those extra ticks are largely unnecessary as long as he is commanding the fastball and manipulating his slider toward the plus range that it routinely flashes. The package is rounded out by a passable changeup he can locate to both sides of the plate with movement. Faedo earns excellent marks for his competitiveness on the mound. He mixes his pitches well and has a chance to walk the fine line that comes with a profile that is more moxie than raw stuff.

Variance: Low. Little is likely to change in Faedo's profile at this point, and as long as nothing regresses significantly, he should be able to handle big league innings every fifth day.

Mark Barry's Fantasy Take: If you look at Faedo's 2019 stats, you might be a little confused as to why he's not getting more buzz. And that's fair—he was incredible in his second spin through Double-A. Even if the numbers have changed, the skills haven't, so it's tough to envision him breaking through as more than a fantasy SP5.

8. Daz Cameron   OF
OFP: 45   ETA: 2020
Born: 01/15/97   Age: 23   Bats: R   Throws: R   Height: 6'2"   Weight: 195
Origin: Round 1, 2015 Draft (#37 overall)

The Report: Cameron has been on the radar for quite some time as the son of a former big leaguer, but his performance has yet to consistently catch up with the name recognition he enjoys. At his best, he shows a broad array of average tools that can play well in game situations. His glove is the most consistent part of his game, with quality defense in center field thanks to above-average speed, an above-average arm, and excellent instincts and feel for the game. He moves well to both sides and reads the ball well off the bat on those hit directly at him. His glove is enough to get him to the big leagues, but the path would be much easier if he were able to make any kind of consistent contact. Cameron's pitch recognition continues to lag behind his instincts in the box, leaving him prone to chasing pitches and leading to too much weak contact. As a result, his average raw power only finds game situations on occasion, leaving his plate appearances too empty, too often, to carve out a regular role. Cameron will need to take advantage of a return trip to Triple-A in order to force his way to Detroit amidst the Tigers rebuild.

Variance: High. The hit tool could go any number of directions, including further off a cliff and completely derailing his future. There's enough other near-average tools to manage a big league role, regardless of the bat, but things get a lot easier if he hits just a little bit.

Mark Barry's Fantasy Take: Learning to hit is hard. Learning to hit against big-league pitching is near impossible. It seems like that's where we're headed with Cameron. He has hit enough in the minors to warrant a look, but with a strikeout rate approaching 30 percent at Triple-A, it will be a tall order to find fantasy usefulness from Cameron, outside of perhaps a handful of steals.

9 Beau Burrows   RHP   OFP: 45   ETA: 2020
Born: 09/18/96   Age: 23   Bats: R   Throws: R   Height: 6'2"   Weight: 215
Origin: Round 1, 2015 Draft (#22 overall)

The Report: Burrows missed significant time on the mound last season due to a variety of injuries, including biceps tendinitis, shoulder inflammation and finally an oblique injury. That lost development time was critical for Burrows as he tried to cement himself as a future rotation workhorse and find his way to the big leagues. Instead, Burrows' command regressed, his changeup failed to progress and whispers of a move to the bullpen grew louder and louder. When healthy, Burrows shows a low-90s fastball that bumps 95-96 mph early in starts. His slider is his best breaking pitch, showing regularly as an above-average mid-80s pitch, while his curveball lacks consistent shape and quality. A below-average changeup completes the pitch mix, though he has yet to discover enough consistency with the change to take the next step. Burrows shows flashes of throwing consistent strikes, but he has yet to move the ball around to the edges of the zone with any regularity. The lack of consistent command and two inconsistent secondary pitches leaves Burrows trending toward the bullpen where he could see a slight tick in power on his fastball and slider, something that would play well in the middle to late innings.

Variance: Medium. Burrows has yet to develop a consistent third pitch or make overwhelming strides with his command, leaving his future in the rotation up in the air. In addition, his ultimate bullpen role is still debatable.

Mark Barry's Fantasy Take: Biceps tendinitis, shoulder inflammation and an oblique injury. Cool, cool, cool. I don't have enough faith in Burrows's stuff to keep him around and wait out his injuries. He's a deep leaguer or AL-only guy that you'll likely find a reasonable facsimile of on the waiver wire.

10 Parker Meadows   OF   OFP: 50   ETA: 2022
Born: 11/02/99   Age: 20   Bats: L   Throws: R   Height: 6'5"   Weight: 205
Origin: Round 2, 2018 Draft (#44 overall)

The Report: The stat line for Meadows took a hit due to some bad luck and a cold Michigan spring, but he still impressed with his raw talent and high upside. There's tons of projection remaining and it's not difficult to see five future above-average tools. The bat's still a ways away from major league ready but it's a pretty left-handed swing that has some natural loft. Physical maturity will bring some natural strength that will make the power play up in game. Meadow's speed and defense will mean the organization will give him plenty of time for the offense to develop. He's not a quick-twitch base stealing threat but there's plus-plus speed which, along with good natural instincts, make him an exceptional base runner. He is also one of the top outfield defenders in the organization, able to handle all three spots. There's a high ceiling in Meadow's profile and a solid 2020 season at High-A Lakeland will catapult him up next year's prospect rankings.

Variance: High. The gap between Meadows' projection and his A-ball performance is significant. On the other side of the coin, you can see the tools flash past this OFP from time to time already.

Mark Barry's Fantasy Take: Meadows is basically his older brother, just more raw and less likely to hit his upside. It's like the reverse Preston/Kyle Tucker dynamic. Even though maximizing his tools might be unlikely, they're still there and they're easy to dream on. We'll know more after this season, but for now, I'm only rostering him in leagues with at least 250 prospects.

The Next Ten

11 Jake Rogers   C
Born: 04/18/95   Age: 25   Bats: R   Throws: R   Height: 6'1"   Weight: 205
Origin: Round 3, 2016 Draft (#97 overall)

Rogers is going to be a backup catcher for a while on the strength of his glove. He's been one of the elite framers in the upper minors and offers a plus arm that will curtail the running game when he's behind the plate. His first pass against major-league arms didn't go so great though. Rogers has some country strong pop, but the combination of a stiff, pull-happy swing and fringe bat speed led to his getting exploited on the outer half of the plate. If he can make some secondary adjustments, he'll run into enough home runs to kick around a major league bench for six or seven years on the strength of the defensive profile.

Detroit Tigers 2020

12   Wilkel Hernandez   RHP
Born: 04/13/99   Age: 21   Bats: R   Throws: R   Height: 6'3"   Weight: 195
Origin: International Free Agent, 2015

Hernandez remains a bit of a project as a pitching prospect, but there's stuff to like here. It's an ideal starter's frame, long and lean, with plenty of projection left. He's smoothed out his delivery and sits low 90s with good run. He has surprising feel for spin given his experience level, and his curveball could grow into an above-average pitch with refinement. His change remains crude however, and he still struggles to hold his velocity into games. He's not starting off in the mid 90s as often either. The shape of the OFP here remains amorphous though, with both fourth starter and bullpen outcomes in play. There's upside past that too, which is why he slots at the top of this run of arms for now. He's also less likely to pitch in the majors at all compared to the names below him. Weight the variance as you see fit.

13   Logan Shore   RHP
Born: 12/28/94   Age: 25   Bats: R   Throws: R   Height: 6'2"   Weight: 215
Origin: Round 2, 2016 Draft (#47 overall)

Shore was arguably the best pitcher on an absolutely loaded 2016 Florida Gators staff. Nowadays he's the seventh-best pitching prospect from that team. Well, technically sixth I guess since their closer, Shaun Anderson, is no longer list-eligible. We often make note of how even your OFP 45 prospects like Shore were usually the best pitcher on their high school and college teams, and occasionally on their minor league teams as well. The Erie rotation was just as loaded as that Gators team, though—and both included Alex Faedo. So it's easy for him to get lost in the shuffle behind Mize, Manning, and Faedo. The stuff won't stand out next to those three, but he offers an effective sinker either side of 90, a potential above-average change, and a potentially average slider. It's very back-of-the-rotation—hence the OFP 45—and he has struggled to miss bats even in Double-A. There may not be much room for him in the Detroit rotation due to...well, Mize, Manning, and Faedo, but a major-league grade is a major-league grade.

14   Kyle Funkhouser   RHP
Born: 03/16/94   Age: 26   Bats: R   Throws: R   Height: 6'2"   Weight: 230
Origin: Round 4, 2016 Draft (#115 overall)

Funkhouser will be 26 before Opening Day 2020 and hasn't thrown 100 innings in a season since 2016. Elbow inflammation in 2017, a freak broken foot in 2018 and a shoulder impingement in 2019 have all limited his time on a professional mound. The scouting report hasn't changed much since I saw him in short-season. He has a fastball he can get up to 95, but sits more 92-94 and runs a little true. The slider is the best secondary now, mid-80s with short, late depth to it. The change is too firm and lacks ideal velocity separation. Control and command issues bubble up too often. The Tigers have used Funkhouser exclusively as a starter as a pro, but it's probably about time to move him to the pen, even if he didn't have durability concerns. The fastball could be more mid 90s when he's airing it out for an inning, and paired with the above-average slider, he could be a perfectly fine fastball/slider middle reliever, maybe even a seventh-inning guy.

15 Franklin Perez   RHP
Born: 12/06/97   Age: 22   Bats: R   Throws: R   Height: 6'3"   Weight: 197
Origin: International Free Agent, 2014

On our 2017 lists, every risk section for every pitching prospect included some variation on "Also, he's a pitcher." The audience got bored with this quickly and moved to actively annoyed later on, but as an Irony Level 5, I'm not going to give up on a bit. There was a broader point to all of it, too. Pitchers are volatile. And you don't know if a pitcher can maintain a workload through a full season, or season over season, until they do it. There's no doubt that Franklin Perez has significantly higher upside than Funkhouser or Shore. You could argue he has more upside than Wentz even now. Perez threw seven innings this year due to shoulder issues. The same barking shoulder limited him to 19 1/3 innings in 2018. There's a chance he never throws a meaningful full professional season again, despite being only 22. That's a downside outcome, but it's in play. The upside outcome is he shows up healthy in 2020 and looks like the dude in Mauricio's report from 2016. But the best predictor of future pitcher injuries is past pitcher injuries, so perhaps you don't want Anton Chigurh flipping that coin.

16 Paul Richan   RHP
Born: 03/26/97   Age: 23   Bats: R   Throws: R   Height: 6'2"   Weight: 200
Origin: Round 2C, 2018 Draft (#78 overall)

Richan, one of the two prospect arms acquired for Nicholas Castellanos, is your standard polished, college strike-thrower. Drafted in the second round by the Cubs out of San Diego in 2018, he throws buckets of strikes with the standard four-pitch mix. The fastball sits in the low 90s but he can move it around the zone and elevate it for Ks when he's ahead. The best of the secondaries is an average slider that has more sweep than tilt, but comes out of the hand like the fastball and offers enough late movement to miss High-A bats. Richan throws a slurvy curve for a different breaking ball look, and a below-average change with occasional fade. It's a good frame, and an easy, repeatable delivery. He has gotten by so far on control and command and may not have an out pitch against better hitters, but so far so good on his road to backend starterdom. Double-A in 2020 will be a stern test of the profile.

17 Nick Quintana   SS
Born: 10/13/97   Age: 22   Bats: R   Throws: R   Height: 5'10"   Weight: 187
Origin: Round 2, 2019 Draft (#47 overall)

Detroit Tigers 2020

The Tigers second-round pick looks a little like an Asylum Films version of Bo Bichette, which is an aesthetic I can get behind. He tries to hit bombs like Bo too, which really isn't his game. There's a big leg kick that hangs in the air for a bit, and a power-hitter swing without the frame or bat speed to back it up. He manages to handle the barrel pretty well despite all of that, and there's some projection in the offensive profile if he can add some strength or calm down some of the swing elements. Quintana looks more athletic in the field than at the plate, showing good hands and lateral range and enough arm for the left side of the infield. He could probably play a fringe shortstop a couple times a week too. He did look pretty gassed by the time he got to Connecticut in August. Forest saw more power potential in the Midwest League earlier in the Summer, so this might be a case of non-representative looks after a long season, but the profile felt more utility infielder than starter.

18 Derek Hill   OF
Born: 12/30/95   Age: 24   Bats: R   Throws: R   Height: 6'2"   Weight: 195
Origin: Round 1, 2014 Draft (#23 overall)

19 Jose Azocar   OF
Born: 05/11/96   Age: 24   Bats: R   Throws: R   Height: 6'0"   Weight: 185
Origin: International Free Agent, 2012

Hill and Azocar make a neatly matched pair in my mind as potential fourth outfielders with some obvious tools, but some obvious warts as well. Hill is the more traditional up-the-middle type, a plus runner with a lean frame and plenty of quick-twitch athleticism. He's a potential plus center fielder so he got the lion's share of the reps there over Azocar, who would likely be fine there and is an above-average runner himself. Azocar has a borderline plus-plus arm though, so naturally he slots into right field more often than not.

At the plate there are issues as both players strike out more than you'd like given both offensive profiles project as hit-over-power. Hill is inconsistent with his setup and hands and struggles with pitches running off the plate. Azocar's setup is very noisy and he's vulnerable to spin and lacks Hill's bat speed. Both are likely extra outfielders in the end.

20 Anthony Castro   RHP
Born: 04/13/95   Age: 25   Bats: R   Throws: R   Height: 6'2"   Weight: 190
Origin: International Free Agent, 2011

Castro has been bouncing around the Tigers system since signing before the 2012 season, all the while showing flashes of intrigue that enticed onlookers. On his best days he runs his fastball up to 97 mph with plenty of life and his slider can miss bats both in and out of the zone. The emergence of an above-average splitfinger has breathed new life into his arsenal and put some shine back on his prospect star. The Tigers tried Castro in the bullpen to start last season before he dazzled as part of a high-profile Erie rotation down the stretch. Castro is a reliever long term and if he can successfully transition to the role throughout 2020, he could be an interesting bullpen piece down the line.

A note about Roberto Campos

Given the shallowness of the organization, and despite my own personal misgivings about aggressively ranking recent J2 signings, this would normally be a system and situation where we'd find a spot for the $2.85 million IFA. Campos provides a particularly difficult time for our evaluation and ranking model however. Even inside the game he was barely known after defecting from Cuba as a 13-year-old. He was largely an unknown quantity while training with ex-Tiger Alex Sanchez in the Dominican. Thus, there is little consensus on where he should have ranked as an IFA even by the specialists in that area, so we will wait until there are more pro looks to go around.

Personal Cheeseball

PC
Jack O'Loughlin   LHP
Born: 03/14/00   Age: 20   Bats: L   Throws: L   Height: 6'5"   Weight: 210
Origin: International Free Agent, 2016

O'Loughlin returned to Norwich this summer looking noticeably slimmer and more athletic and with a few more ticks on the fastball to boot. It now sits either side of 90, with some sink and run at the high end and a distinct cutter at the low. There's deception from the cross-body mechanics, although he's smoothed out the control and command issues somewhat. The curve improved as well, ticking up to the mid 70s with more consistent 1-7 break that he could get gloveside or backdoor. The change shows a circle and split look with 10 mph of velocity separation off the fastball. He's more comfortable throwing the split in on righties and he will lean on the pitch heavily, although it only has an average projection. O'Loughlin is still a teenager, and while he lacks projection in both body and stuff, and the delivery has some effort and whack to it, the year-over-year improvements are a good marker. And I'm still a sucker for a lefty with a fun change.

Low Minors Sleeper

LMS
Ryan Kreidler   SS
Born: 11/12/97   Age: 22   Bats: R   Throws: R   Height: 6'4"   Weight: 208
Origin: Round 4, 2019 Draft (#112 overall)

After my first couple of looks at Kreidler, I wrote "feels like a Mets fourth-round pick" in my notebook. That is not a compliment given the Mets' lack of success with Day Two college bats over the last, oh, decade or so. He grew on me over the course of subsequent games. The collection of tools are mostly on the fringy side of average, but he gets it done at short and will show some ability to stay inside the ball and use all fields. He struggled a bit with spin at times and there is below-average power production at best, as his contact can lack oomph despite average bat speed. Kreidler has a little less projection and athleticism than Quintana, but looked like the better player at present.

Top Talents 25 and Under (as of 4/1/2020)

1. Casey Mize
2. Matt Manning
3. Riley Greene
4. Tarik Skubal
5. Joey Wentz
6. Joe Jimenez
7. Isaac Paredes
8. Alex Faedo
9. Daz Cameron
10. Victor Reyes

We could easily copy-paste the prospects list and be done here, and not a jury of editors in the tri-state area would convict. Still.

A team this far into a generational cryogenic nap usually transitions the first call-ups from a status of "this will be interesting to see" to "no not like that," and Jake Rogers, a top 10 talent last year, literally hit .125 in two months with the Tigers and missed the cut. Likewise, 26-year-old Jeimer Candelario graduates, but unfortunately with a philosophy degree, hence the lack of a guaranteed job for 2020.

The Packard plant blossom in this garden is Jimenez. One would think he would have recorded more than 12 saves by now. He ought to double it this season and his career should go another five years. He's the same age as Joel Zumaya when his arm could no longer generate velocity, so the habitual eye-rolling on all paragraphs with respect to budding Tigers relievers are understandable. Hence, he'll age off the list a success story.

That leaves us with two options: comprise the 25U list with prospects plus Jimenez or throw a bone to one of those young deer in the headlights who merely got nicked by a side mirror, and that was Reyes. He was an easy out during his 2018 Rule 5 stash year but progressed on all his strengths (contact, baserunning, defense). He's a corner outfielder who can't hit home runs, which is a dying species for a reason. But his 89 DRC+ was a better metric than anyone else in his dugout's age bracket. It wasn't a bright spot, nor a reason for hope. But it definitely happened.

For Detroit, the prospect list started out ghastly. Then the entire major league roster was housed inside Janet's boundless void. Now it's this list. Before you know it, the growing pains will properly shift to all these promising right-handers in the major league rotation, getting early showers thanks to [checks notes] the Royals, again.

Part 3: Featured Articles

The Baseball Is Juiced (Again)

Robert Arthur

This article originally appeared at Baseball Prospectus on April 5, 2019.

It started when the normally reliable Chris Sale got lit up for three homers by the Mariners in the Red Sox's season opener. It was part of a record number of taters that flew on Opening Day, as starters from Sale to Zack Greinke were taken deep by the handful. Then Christian Yelich hit a home run in each of his first four games, tying yet another MLB record, this one for consecutive games with a dinger to start a season.

It didn't take long for fans and players to begin whispering and tweeting about the baseballs being juiced again. It's early yet for us to come to any definitive conclusion about the 2019 season, but preliminary data shows that the baseball has returned to its aerodynamic peak. Whether that means this season will smash home run records like 2017 did remains to be seen.

Before home run explosion over the last few years, no one worried too much about the baseball's air resistance. While MLB and Rawlings (the company that manufactures the official baseballs) kept track of dozens of metrics to make sure that the ball was consistent from month to month, they didn't measure drag.

But drag is incredibly important in determining how likely a hitter is to knock one out of the park. As baseballs become more aerodynamic, they travel further given a certain initial velocity. A deep fly ball that might have been caught at the warning track can instead go into the first row of the stands. A three percent change in drag coefficient can work to add about five feet to a well-hit fly ball, which can in turn increase home runs league wide by an astounding 10-15 percent.

It's possible to measure the aerodynamics of the baseball using the pitch-tracking radars currently in place in each MLB ballpark. By calculating the loss of speed from when the pitch is released to when it crosses the plate, you can directly measure the drag coefficient on the baseball. I first wrote about the role of decreasing drag in boosting home runs in 2017, and MLB's commission of scientists and statisticians later confirmed that the more aerodynamic baseballs in use that year were largely to blame for the spike in home runs. The same commission rejected some alternate hypotheses, like rising temperatures and a league-wide boost in launch angle pushing more balls over the fence.

The current era has featured some large fluctuations in drag coefficient, leading to first an explosion in 2016 and 2017, and then a dialing back of homers last year. Curious about the record-breaking home run tallies in the last few days, I used the same methodology to measure the aerodynamics of the baseballs so far in 2019.

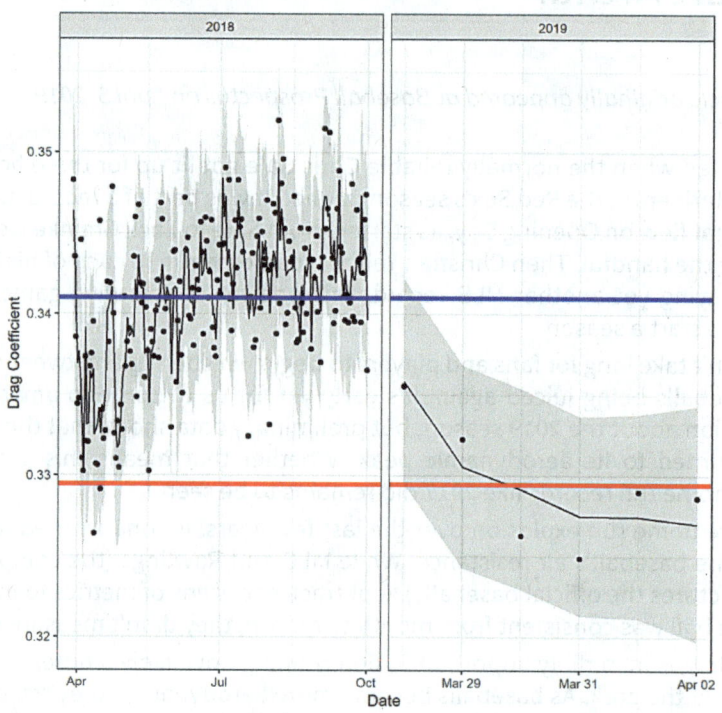

We're only a week into the 2019 season, but the drag numbers so far are among the lowest recorded in the last calendar year. With apologies for gory math, the current 2019 season average drag coefficient (the red line) would be below the 95 percent credible interval (the shaded area) for about nine-tenths of the 2018 season. (I used a Bayesian Random Walk model implemented in INLA to calculate these credible intervals, averaging the drag numbers in each game and adjusting for park.)

There were only a handful of six-day stretches in 2018 that had drag numbers below what we're seeing now, and most were in late June and early July. All of this means that 2019's data so far is quite a bit different than what we saw through most of last year.

These drag coefficients factor out the effects of temperature and air density, so they aren't a product of April cold. However, the numbers could be deceptive if the radars used to track pitches have changed from year to year. I consulted with some experts within baseball who were not aware of any specific modifications to the radar this year that could produce this pattern, but it's an important caveat of which to be aware.

On the one hand, it's only been six days, and we don't quite have the statistical basis to say that these drag coefficients are unprecedented compared to 2018. On the other hand, we've witnessed about 5,000 fastballs so far this season, so it's not as if our sample size is small. At least so far, the baseball has played like it's much more aerodynamic than it was last year. In fact, the current drag coefficient is really only comparable to 2017, when the baseballs were more aerodynamic than they had been in at least a decade.

It's not just fancy radar tracking indicating that the baseball is flying through the air more easily. The current number of home runs per game (as of this writing) is the highest it's been since the heady days of 2017, the year that teams and players broke dinger-related records everywhere you looked. That's especially remarkable considering that we're in what is typically the coldest part of the regular season, when lower temperatures and higher winds tend to suppress offense and keep balls in the air within the park. Comparing only from April to April, this year's rate of home runs per fly ball is even a little bit higher than it was in 2017.

With that said, the current measurements are no guarantee that 2019 will be another year of record-shattering homer hitting. The trouble with the drag measurements is that they are not consistent from June to August, from week to week, or even sometimes from day to day. Whether because of natural manufacturing variation or differences in the underlying supplies of cowhide and thread that go into the baseballs, drag has a tendency to fluctuate up and down over the course of a year. So the homers that fly in the first week of April wouldn't necessarily clear the fence a week later.

It's possible that this one-week drop in drag coefficient subsides and the baseball returns to its 2018 levels. On the other hand, it's almost equally probable that the ball becomes even more slippery and flies ever farther. Either way, it's clear that the baseball's air resistance is something to keep an eye on for the remainder of the 2019 season.

—*Robert Arthur is an author of Baseball Prospectus.*

The Moral Hazard of Playing It Safe

Craig Goldstein

This article originally appeared at Baseball Prospectus on August 6, 2019.

A couple days prior to the trade deadline, amidst a sea of tranquility posing as the lead up to the trade deadline, Bob Nightengale took to Twitter. Nightengale, who was probably wearing his pants backwards at the time, tweeted that MLB GMs were coming around on the idea that the unified trade deadline should be moved back from July 31 to August 15, so they could better assess their positions in the standings and whether they should buy or sell. To which I said:

This might strike some as reductive and churlish. And it might be that, but it isn't really wrong, either. Jeff Quinton wrote a great piece discussing the environmental factors that enable front offices to avoid risk without upsetting the apple cart within their own fanbases. I don't believe that it goes far enough, however. His article gives us the proper framework through which to understand why these behaviors have been allowed to seep into front offices throughout the league. Understanding the reasons behind these actions are different from excusing them, though, and GMs should not be let off the hook for their non-competitive approach to the trade deadline (much less the offseason).

⚾ ⚾ ⚾

It's fair to say that fans as a group have rarely, if ever, been pro-player. It is also fair to say that in the time during and following the Moneyball revolution, the pendulum swung from fans who cared intensely about winning in the moment (and thus might be intolerant of a rebuilding approach) to fans who supported building a team that could compete throughout multiple seasons, viewing the playoffs as a crapshoot, with the thought that getting multiple bites at the apple was a better approach than taking a bigger bite in any one season.

There's nothing wrong with that approach, and I still find merit in that argument. However, it seems that the pendulum has swung too far in that direction. Teams are overvaluing some of the individual factors that make themselves long-term contenders rather than attempting to seize a championship when given the opportunity. It's a difficult needle to thread.

And surely, they (and those in similar positions) would have liked another two weeks to clarify where they stand so as to better marshal their resources. We've all asked for a few more minutes when staring at a menu. But all of these GMs and front office personnel are where they are to make difficult decisions. They have proprietary data and internal analysts dedicated to understanding their position relative to the rest of the league, and how any move in the here and now impacts their long-term vision. To complain (if that report is accurate) that over half the season is not enough to properly assess their season is bullshit of the highest order. Move the deadline, and you'd simply have increasingly discounted trade offers because teams would be acquiring even less control of anyone they're acquiring, rental or not.

Major league front offices are behaving like the managers they lampooned two decades ago. They're effectively sacrificing a runner to second in the ninth inning—not because it's the correct move, but rather because it is safe. It used to be that the phrase "moral hazard" was used to describe general managers who made ill-fated, short-sighted decisions aimed at locking in wins and securing their jobs at the expense of their team's future. Now, general managers are guilty of committing moral hazards in the opposite direction, playing it utterly safe and terrified of becoming scapegoats.

In lieu of bold action, they opt to pussyfoot around a current window of contention, choosing instead to play the long game and stack up years of control like they're blocks in a game of Jenga. GMs pass on signing quality players in free agency because the back-end of the deal might look bad, and because they might be able to squeeze out 70 percent of the production from a player who costs a tenth as much. That's a safer investment, too, because it's also hard to prove a negative—it's impossible to prove that Manny Machado would make the Mets a playoff team in 2019-2020, but it's easy to say that the back half of Robinson Cano's contract sucks. Owners, who rule over GM's jobs, are also humans with human brain processes that will always make the so-called albatross contract uglier than the road not taken.

These days, GMs are remembered for the bad deals they make and the surplus value they generate, not the acquisition of expensive, necessary talents that meet their market worth (or fall slightly short while still providing significant on-field value). And front offices know that one or two expensive misfires can cost them their jobs, no matter how many good deals they make.

No front office exemplifies this ethos more than the Toronto Blue Jays. General Manager Ross Atkins had this to say following the Blue Jays underwhelming trade deadline:

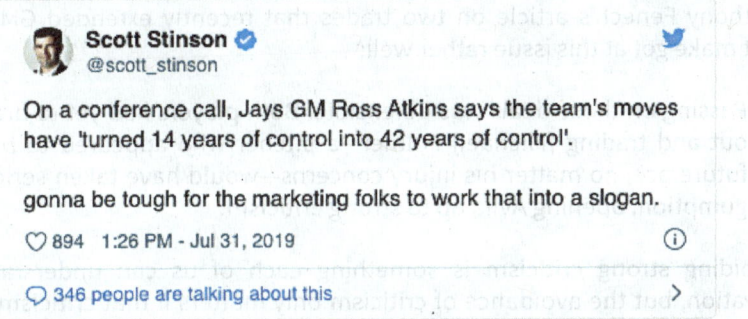

This is by no means the first time that an executive will cite years of control to justify their actions, which is often just another way of saying "don't look at what we got, look at how much we got of it." Atkins touts quantity to elide the discussion of quality—either, that of the players acquired, or those given up. Remember: the other teams presumably value years of control, too.

Atkins also had some thoughts to offer regarding free agents back in early 2018:

This ignores, of course, whether the player can create enough value in the front end of a contract to justify the longer term of a deal, and the decline that often occurs in the back end. It also ignores whether the player can fill a need the team requires and put them in a position to compete for and win a championship. But as teams seemingly avoid contention at all, where they might end up having to consider and later justify some of these tough decisions, we still see risk-averse approaches.

Anthony Fenech's article on two trades that recently extended GM Al Avila didn't make got at this issue rather well:

> Passing on those deals was defensible: Both players had yet to break out and trading [Michael] Fulmer—a pitcher who appeared to be a future ace, no matter his injury concerns—would have taken serious gumption, opening Avila up to strong criticism.

Avoiding strong criticism is something each of us can understand as a motivation, but the avoidance of criticism only matters if that criticism is valid. In Fulmer's case, shoving his injury concerns aside affects not only the years that the team controls him (he is currently missing a full season due to Tommy John surgery) but also the quality of those seasons, as his knee and elbow injuries combined to dampen his effectiveness even when healthy enough to pitch. But it was easy to present the then-current image of Fulmer as a top of the rotation pitcher who the team had under its domain for the next five seasons as something to build around. The status quo isn't nearly as often second-guessed as a decision that disrupts it.

⚾ ⚾ ⚾

MLB GMs are risk-averse to a fault. They are ivy-educated and consulting firm-approved, and yet they can't seem to avoid leaving wins on the table in their all-consuming lust for a non-existent $/WAR championship. They are supposed to zig when everyone else zags, and not merely pay lip service to the idea of zigging through a calculated PR plan built on convincing the fan base their approach is novel when it actually apes most of their competitors. Instead they've become far more concerned with making safe, accepted-by-the-new-common-wisdom decisions, such that our prior understanding of what a moral hazard is has become inverted.

I can't blame them entirely, and not only because of the reasons that Quinton illuminated in his article, but also because of the damage wrought by the introduction of the second wild card (WC2) spot. MLB's desire to have more teams in playoff contention has sparked anti-competitive behavior. Teams know now that they do not need to swing big as they assemble their roster because there is a good chance that a mediocre team can either catch fire and capture a division, or muddle along until they back into the WC2.

Simultaneously, the one-game playoff has neutered the WC1, putting an entire season on the flip of a coin like some sort of baseball-obsessed Anton Chigurh. While the one-game playoff makes sense as a way to increase the value of winning a division, it also means that if a front office doesn't like its chances of overcoming a behemoth like the Dodgers or Astros in the offseason, they have few incentives to chase glory. Similarly, the relative inaction in the NL Central at the trade deadline—despite a wide open division—can be explained by the idea that any high-variance investment could still result in only a wild card (or worse) result, given the mere two months left in the season to make an impact.

⚾ ⚾ ⚾

As stated at the top, we should not confuse reasons for excuses. The implementation of the second wild card is just one of many environmental factors that influence how each front office operates. I am convinced that it is one of the larger factors, but I am also convinced that organizations need to shed the yoke of "efficiency at all costs" so that they can instead pursue competition, as the spirit of the game intends. Until they do, we're all deadline losers.

—*Craig Goldstein is an author of Baseball Prospectus.*

Index of Names

Adams, Austin 100
Agrazal, Dario 56
Alcantara, Sergio 98
Alcantara, Victor 100
Alexander, Tyler 58
Azocar, Jose 112
Baez, Sandy 100
Beckham, Gordon 18
Bonifacio, Jorge 98
Boyd, Matthew 60
Burrows, Beau 89, 108
Cabrera, Miguel 20
Cameron, Daz 84, 107
Campos, Roberto 85
Candelario, Jeimer 22
Carpenter, Ryan 100
Castro, Anthony 100, 112
Castro, Harold 24
Castro, Willi 26
Cisnero, Jose 62
Cron, C.J. 28
Demeritte, Travis 30
Dixon, Brandon 32
Faedo, Alex 90, 107
Farmer, Buck 64
Fernandez, Jose 100
Fulmer, Michael 91
Funkhouser, Kyle 100, 110
Garcia, Bryan 100
Garcia, Rony 100
Godley, Zack 66
Goodrum, Niko 34
Greene, Riley 86, 104
Greiner, Grayson 36
Guzman, Carlos 100
Haase, Eric 98
Hall, Matt 100
Hernandez, Wilkel 100, 110
Hill, Derek 98, 112
Jimenez, Eduardo 100
Jiménez, Joe 68
Jones, JaCoby 38
Kozma, Pete 98
Kreidler, Ryan 113
Lange, Alex 100
Lugo, Dawel 40
Manning, Matt 92, 104
Maybin, Cameron 42
McKay, David 100
Meadows, Parker 98, 109
Mercer, Jordy 44
Mize, Casey 93, 103
Moore, Matt 94
Norris, Daniel 70
Nova, Iván 72
Numata, Chace 87
O'Loughlin, Jack 113
Paredes, Isaac 88, 106
Perez, Franklin 95, 111
Perez, Wenceel 98
Peterson, Dustin 98
Quintana, Nick 98, 111

Detroit Tigers 2020

Ramirez, Nick 74
Reininger, Zac 101
Reyes, Victor 46
Richan, Paul 101, 111
Robson, Jacob 98
Rodriguez, Elvin 101
Rogers, Jake 48, 109
Romine, Austin 50
Schoop, Jonathan 52
Schreiber, John 101
Schwindel, Frank 98
Shore, Logan 110

Skubal, Tarik 96, 105
Soto, Gregory 76
Stewart, Christin 54
Stokes, Troy 98
Stumpf, Daniel 101
Turnbull, Spencer 78
VerHagen, Drew 80
Wentz, Joey 97, 106
Wilson, Alex 101
Wilson, Bobby 98
Zimmermann, Jordan 82